20
COMPELLING
EVIDENCES THAT
GOD EXISTS

Discover Why Believing in God
Makes So Much Sense

Kenneth D. Boa
and
Robert M. Bowman Jr.

RIVER
OAK
PUBLISHING

20 Compelling Evidences That God Exists
ISBN 1-58919-306-7
Copyright © 2002 by Kenneth Boa and Robert Bowman

Published by RiverOak Publishing,
a Division of Cook Communications Ministries
P.O. Box 55388
Tulsa, Oklahoma 74155

20
COMPELLING EVIDENCES THAT GOD EXISTS

Contents

Foreword

What? Begin with doubts?

Well, yes, of course—if that's where you honestly are.

We can speak from experience here. We've struggled in the past with doubts too. We wondered if there really was a God and if He cared about us. When we first heard about the God of the Bible, we weren't sure if we could believe it. The whole thing seemed so—fantastic. Frankly, we wanted some evidence. We didn't buy into the Christian message without first becoming convinced that there were some very good reasons to believe it.

So, if you're not sure what to believe and you want some evidence that Christianity isn't just a nice uplifting myth, we can relate. In this book, we offer twenty evidences supporting belief in God. We think these evidences are compelling. But whatever you do, don't take our word for it. Consider the arguments, investigate the evidence, check out our facts, seek out alternate opinions—do whatever you need to do to settle the issue in your own mind. We assume that you're at a point in your life where you are open to the evidence and want to know whether God is real or not. If that's the case, the evidence presented in this book should be of interest to you.

Before we go any further, it might be helpful to tell you the kinds of reasons that we will *not* be giving for belief in God. We don't claim that believing in God will make you more successful or wealthy. Unfortunately, every religion has its hucksters—people who try to turn that religion into a way to bilk people out of their money—and Christianity is no exception. Don't let such people distract you from getting at the truth of whether or not God is real.

All of the twenty evidences we discuss in this book pertain to showing that the God of the Bible—the God who created us and who has demonstrated His love for us in Jesus Christ—really exists. These evidences are not, by the way, the findings of our own "undercover investigation" into the existence of God. (Beware of the person who assures you that he has finally, for the first time in human history, discovered proof that God exists!) They are more like signs that God himself has posted to show people where to find Him and that many people, we ourselves included, have found to be personally compelling pointers to God.

When we describe these evidences as "compelling," then, we don't mean that everyone will be bowled over by our explanation of every bit of evidence or that we have made such a definitive and irrefutable case for these evidences that no one will be able to resist the conclusion that God exists. The evidences are compelling in and of themselves, but our articulation of those evidences will only be as good as our grasp on them. On the other hand, if someone doesn't *want* to believe in God, no amount of evidence can force such a person to accept God's existence as fact. Furthermore, because people are different, certain points will probably weigh more heavily with you than others. That's OK. There is only one God, but there are many evidences that support belief in Him—more, in fact, than we discuss in this book.

We should also note that some of these evidences for God are compelling only in conjunction with other evidences. If a particular piece of evidence is isolated from the others and treated abstractly as a single point, it may lose its punch. That being the case, you should know that the later chapters build to a considerable extent on the earlier chapters.

Feel free to skip around if you like; just keep in mind that we have tried to present these evidences in a helpful order.

> THE WHOLE HISTORY OF HUMANITY AS SUCH CAN BE WRITTEN AS A SEARCH FOR A MEANINGFUL ANSWER TO THE QUESTION OF THE EXISTENCE OF GOD.
> —TERRY L. MIETHE AND GARY R. HABERMAS[2]

Before we launch into our discussion of the evidences for God, we need to clarify a couple of things. Our goal here is not merely to provide evidences that support believing in *a* God. In other words, we're not just trying to disprove atheism. Our focus in this book is on evidences supporting belief in *God*. This God is someone real—someone we want you to know.

The easiest way for us to tell you about this God is to tell you the story of what He has done. It is a story already familiar to many. God created the universe and designed it as a place for us to live. He made life and brought the human race into existence. He thinks of us as children, wanting to love us and give us everything but also expecting us to live by His rules. When we turned away from Him, He acted to restore our relationship with Him. He revealed himself to Abraham and his descendants, created the nation of Israel as a special people through whom He would make himself known to the rest of the world, and gave them His laws and His wisdom. Then, when the time was right, He sent His Son into the world to live as a human being. His name was Jesus. He healed the sick, performed other miracles, taught about His Father, and spoke out against the hypocrisy in His own people's religion. He was put to death on a cross and three days later rose from the dead. Before going back to Heaven, Jesus told those who believed in Him to tell others what had happened and what it meant. His death, which they had thought was a terrible tragedy, was actually the means by which God was bringing human beings back into a relationship with Him. His resurrection was the proof that God had sent Him and the beginning of new, eternal life for all who believe in Him. Jesus' followers have been spreading this message ever since, in some instances at the cost of their lives. It is a message of hope for all people.

This is the God we want you to know. He is infinitely deserving of your time, of your trust, and of your love. But again, don't take our word for it. Consider the evidence for yourself.

1

THE EVIDENCE *of* REALITY

IF A BELIEF SYSTEM DOESN'T CLAIM
TO CORRESPOND TO REALITY, HEAD
FOR THE NEAREST EXIT!

We don't mean to discourage you from reading the rest of this book; but in the interest of full disclosure, we should tell you that, in a sense, there is only one good reason to believe that God exists: *because it's true.*

Throughout this book, we will be presenting evidence for the existence of the God of the Bible. There are many such evidences, but they all have value because they help us see that the God of the Bible is *real.*

The moment we bring reality or truth into the discussion about God, though, many people get uncomfortable. Ask who won the World Series in 1961 or what percentage of the American population is sixty-five years of age or older or how to get a rocket to the moon, and everybody expects sober answers that relate to the real world. Gasoline, not lemonade, goes in the fuel tank of your car; we would all view a person as crazy who thought that it was a "personal lifestyle choice" to put lemonade in his car and drink gasoline. In most matters, most people speak and act as if reality matters. But not when it comes to God. Somehow, in matters of religion, spirituality, faith, or God, people have this idea that it doesn't matter what you believe, as long as you're sincere and don't hurt people. In fact, many people are troubled by claims that a particular religious belief is actually true— that it corresponds to reality—and is not merely the subjective feeling or point of view of those who believe it.

What could be behind this notion? Here is one possibility: The idea that no religious belief can claim to express reality could presuppose that there is no religious reality to know. For example, the idea that religious beliefs about God cannot claim to correspond to reality might presuppose that there is no real God at all. If this were true, then God would not really exist. Rather, God would be a myth or symbol, the ultimate Imaginary Friend. When people pray to God, they would in actuality be talking to themselves. God would be at best a comforting lie, something people believe in because it helps them escape from reality.

Frankly, if we thought there was any truth to this view of God, we wouldn't bother you with evidences supporting belief in Him. For that matter, we wouldn't bother believing in God ourselves. We have absolutely no use for escapist religion. If God doesn't really exist, we should close up all of the churches and turn them into cinemas or bowling alleys or libraries. Our only interest in Christianity is in whether it can deliver on its promises—and what Christianity promises cannot happen unless Christianity is true. As C. S. Lewis put it:

Christianity is not a patent medicine. Christianity claims to give an account of facts—to tell you what the real universe is like. Its account of the universe may be true, or it may not, and once the question is really before you, then your natural inquisitiveness must make you want to know the answer. If Christianity is untrue, then no honest man will want to believe it, however helpful it might be: if it is true, every honest man will want to believe it, even if it gives him no help at all.[1]

You might be wondering why Lewis would say something like this. Can't Christianity be a positive, helpful religion even if it's not literally true? And why believe in it if it isn't helpful? The answer is that

Christianity ultimately claims one thing: to tell us what the real, living God has done to bring us back into a relationship with Him that will last beyond the grave for all eternity. If this God doesn't even exist, obviously, the whole thing is just a sham. Yes, some people might find some "help" in believing a lie, but that isn't the right way to live. On the other hand, if this God does exist and you believe in Him, you are not guaranteed immediate entrance into a thornless rose garden. So, the only things that really matter here are whether Christianity is true and whether the God of the Christian faith really exists.

THERE'S NO ESCAPE

I REFUSE TO BE INTIMIDATED BY REALITY ANYMORE.... MY SPACE CHUMS THINK REALITY WAS ONCE A PRIMITIVE METHOD OF CROWD CONTROL THAT GOT OUT OF HAND.... I MADE SOME STUDIES, AND REALITY IS THE LEADING CAUSE OF STRESS AMONG THOSE IN TOUCH WITH IT. I CAN TAKE IT IN SMALL DOSES, BUT AS A LIFESTYLE I FOUND IT TOO CONFINING.

—LILY TOMLIN AS TRUDY IN *THE SEARCH FOR SIGNS OF INTELLIGENT LIFE IN THE UNIVERSE*[2]

In the popular science-fiction movie *The Matrix*, Keanu Reeves plays an ordinary man who is not ordinary at all. But then, everything that *seems* ordinary turns out not to be real. Reeves' character, called Neo—a tip-off that he is the first of a new kind of man—learns that his whole world is actually a "virtual reality" illusion called "the Matrix" that was created by alien machines that have taken over the Earth. He and the rest of humanity have been living a lie. At first the truth is very hard to accept, and Neo finds it difficult to make the transition from the "virtual" world to the "real" world.

The Matrix is an enjoyable and thought-provoking film on many levels. There is, however, one way to ruin it entirely, and that is to take it too seriously. Like much science fiction, *The Matrix* is best understood as a parable.[3] Its point is not that alien machines might exist or that virtual reality might one day supplant living in the real world (although many people take both speculations seriously today). At its heart, the film provokes the viewer to consider the possibility that reality is larger than the familiar material world that we experience through our five senses. But it would be a big mistake to take the scenario depicted in the film literally.

On one level, *The Matrix* and countless films like it are tools of escapism. They provide for their viewers an opportunity to "escape" from the "real" world into a cinematic virtual reality where life is more exciting, more romantic, or in some other way more enjoyable than their ordinary lives. Good escapist films give us an emotional boost that helps us get back to our daily routines with more enthusiasm. In that way, escapism in the movies (or in books or television) is not really about escaping reality but about strengthening us to deal with reality.

While escapism in the movies is fun and generally harmless, escapism in worldviews, philosophies, or religions is foolish and can be very harmful indeed. There's no point in trying to avoid the truth about who and what we are or why we're here in this world. If there is a God who made us and who expects something of us, we need to know. If God is nothing more than make-believe, on the level of Santa Claus or the tooth fairy, we need to know that too.

That reality exists and is inescapable can be illustrated using *The Matrix.* In the story line, the "reality" is that the machines have taken over the planet and the "lives" that Neo and his human friends have been living are virtual-reality fiction. When Neo learns this to be the reality of his world, he does not conclude that *nothing* is real but that what he had thought was real was merely an illusion. The very concept of an illusion presupposes a reality, since an illusion is a distortion or deception that hides the way things really are. At some point one must reach a "bottom line," a place where the illusion ends and nothing but reality remains. Thus, reality must exist, and ultimately we cannot escape it.

FAITH FOUNDED ON FACT

There are many religions in the marketplace of ideas. Why believe in one rather than another? Let us begin by narrowing the field down to those we can take seriously. Here's a suggestion: Start by eliminating all religions that show a disregard for facts in the real world. Suppose we were to invite you to believe in the Great Pumpkin.[6] Naturally, you would begin asking questions about matters of fact: Has anyone ever seen the Great Pumpkin? Did he ever leave you candy? Suppose that we not only had no facts about the Great Pumpkin to offer you, but we dismissed your questions as irrelevant and irreverent. If we told you, "The Great Pumpkin comes only to those who ask no questions," would you take Pumpkinism seriously? Of course not. But for some odd reason, people often accept this sort of contempt for reality in religion. Many religions encourage their members to base their beliefs on their *feeling* that it is true. Other religions base their claims on tradition—"We've passed these stories down for centuries," they say, "and they're part of our heritage."

Please understand: we're not knocking feelings or tradition. They are both important elements of human existence, and we can't function well without them. Our point is that it is the job of neither feelings nor tradition to serve as the basis for accepting a belief. A belief should be embraced because it's true—because it's based on reality.

Christianity is one of the few religions that even professes to be grounded on facts in the real world—factual claims that you can read about, investigate, and that are well supported by evidence. It is also a religion that believes it is possible for humans to know these facts and to be held accountable for their response to them. As John Warwick Montgomery put it, Christianity is a "faith founded on fact."[5]

The simple believes every word,
But the prudent considers well his steps.
—PROVERBS 14:15 NKJV

Many people are surprised to hear that Christianity puts so much stock in fact. The Bible, however, is very clear on the matter. The Book of Proverbs warns repeatedly against naivete (Proverbs 1:22; 8:5; 14:15, 18; 22:3) and urges its readers to acquire knowledge (Proverbs 2:10; 8:9; 10:14; 12:1). "The truth," Jesus said, "shall make you free" (John 8:32 KJV). Luke and John both insisted that what they reported about Jesus was historical fact (Luke 1:1-4; John 19:34-35; 21:24). The apostles warned against believing fables or myths (1 Timothy 1:4; 4:7; 2 Timothy 4:3-4; Titus 1:14) and stated confidently that their message was based on fact (Acts 26:26; 2 Peter 1:16).

Christianity, then, unlike many religions, encourages critical questions, discourages naivete, and offers factual reasons or evidences to believe its astounding claims. The very nature of these claims—that God entered our physical reality and left concrete footprints in history—is a basic, fundamental reason to take those claims seriously. This first evidence—that Christianity takes reality seriously—does not prove that Christianity alone is true, but it does put it in the realm of options for serious truth seekers. Whether it is true or not must be determined by considering more specific evidences. If those evidences hold up, the only reasonable thing to do is to believe in the God of the Bible.

But wait a minute! Even if there is such a thing as reality, is it possible for us to know what that reality truly is? Is knowledge of truth possible? That's the question that will occupy our attention next.

For Further Reading

Boa, Kenneth D., and Robert M. Bowman Jr. *Faith Has Its Reasons: An Integrative Approach to Defending Christianity.* Colorado Springs: NavPress, 2001. In this book we explain the different ways Christians for the past two millennia have gone about showing that Christianity is reasonable, and we explain how those different approaches complement one another.

Moreland, J. P. *Love God with All Your Mind: The Role of Reason in the Life of the Soul.* Colorado Springs: NavPress, 2001. Why the Christian faith encourages the cultivation of critical thinking skills.

2
THE EVIDENCE *of* KNOWLEDGE

You will know the truth, and
the truth will set you free.
—JESUS CHRIST (JOHN 8:32 NLT)

Obviously, *The Matrix* is fiction, not fact. Or is it? Some people see a
film like *The Matrix* and ask how we can know that the world we see is,
in fact, real. They understand the film to be suggesting that we cannot
know for sure what the nature of reality is.

It is possible to imagine any number of scenarios in which everything we think we know is untrue. Rod Serling's television series *The*
Twilight Zone explored such scenarios in a thought-provoking and enter-

taining fashion. Because there is no way to "prove" indisputably that we are not, for example, the playthings of an extremely large child, some people conclude that anything is possible and therefore we cannot be sure that we know anything.

The notion that we cannot know anything or that we cannot be sure of anything is much older than twentieth-century science fiction. It is at least as old as the ancient Greek philosophers, many of whom embraced it. In philosophy, this notion is called *skepticism*. A consistent or thoroughgoing skeptic questions everything and professes not to know anything.

THE NEW SKEPTICISM

Although skepticism is very old, in the late twentieth century a rather new form of skepticism emerged that is still shaking things up. This new form of skepticism is called *postmodernism*. Fittingly, nobody really knows what postmodernism is. (We couldn't resist!) Actually, the meaning of postmodernism is almost as fiercely debated as its value. Rather than offer a technical review of that debate, we'll summarize four of the most notable characteristics of postmodernist thought, comparing it to the early-twentieth-century modernist thought that preceded it.

Power controls knowledge. According to postmodernists, all knowledge is political. That is to say, what people believe is shaped largely by their relationship to the political powers that govern the institutions (such as schools and churches) through which knowledge is transmitted. Whereas modernists want to free the pursuit and transmission of knowledge from political control (say, through democratic reforms), postmodernists want to gain political power for communities (e.g., religions, races, or cultures) whose views have been "suppressed" or "underrepresented." As postmodernists see it, since knowledge can never be free from political control, the solution is for each community to seek whatever power it can to preserve and extend its voice.

Objectivity is dead. Postmodernists argue that the goal of a perspective-free, objective view of reality must be abandoned. Modernists recognize that people have different perspectives, or ways of looking at the same things, but seek to overcome those differences through reason. They typically think that humans can achieve a neutral, impartial, "objective," and total view of reality through the rigorous application of logic and the scientific method. Postmodernists regard such a goal as neither realistic nor desirable. In their view, neutrality is unattainable: it is impossible, even in science, to approach any subject matter with no preconceived notions, no presuppositions, and no point of view. Postmodernists also view neutrality as undesirable: different cultures, different religions, and other types of communities have different perspectives that give them their identity. Postmodernists contend that these different perspectives should be celebrated and preserved, not challenged or critiqued.

Science constructs models; it does not describe reality. The goal of science as understood in modernism is a comprehensive knowledge of the world as it really is. In contrast, Thomas Kuhn's 1962 landmark book *The Structure of Scientific Revolutions* itself led a revolution in science.[1] According to Kuhn, science constructs models or *paradigms*— idealized representations of the way things are in the world—and these paradigms approach but never correspond to or arrive at an objective truth. Rather, they are replaced from time to time as the need arises, typically from the introduction of new information that the old paradigm cannot easily support. Kuhn has convinced a generation that science cannot and need not seek truth; its goal is rather an understanding of nature that meets the needs of the scientific community and of the larger society. Such a view of science, of course, implies that scientific theories are now to be assessed partly in terms of how well they support the values of those who pursue science.

Tolerance, not truth, is absolute. Modernists value tolerance, partly in the belief that by tolerating all points of view, we have a better chance of arriving at truth. In modernism, tolerance means *accepting people of different beliefs* even while feeling free to disagree with those beliefs. Postmodernists, on the other hand, value tolerance *over* truth. The postmodernist understands tolerance to mean *accepting people's different beliefs* and therefore refraining from criticizing or even disagreeing with those beliefs. Postmodernists are especially bothered by claims that a particular religious or ethical belief is *the truth* that all people ought to accept. Rather than examining such claims to see whether they hold up in light of the facts, postmodernists dismiss such claims as arrogant, narrow-minded, and intolerant.

These four elements of postmodern thought can be remembered using the acrostic *POST:*

POWER CONTROLS KNOWLEDGE.
OBJECTIVITY IS DEAD.
SCIENCE CONSTRUCTS MODELS;
IT DOES NOT DESCRIBE REALITY.
TOLERANCE, NOT TRUTH, IS ABSOLUTE.

ANSWERING POSTMODERNISM

Postmodernism does not present you with a take-it-or-leave-it proposition. You don't have to choose between accepting it and rejecting it wholesale. We think it's possible to appreciate many of the concerns and insights in postmodernism without subscribing to it uncritically. In this regard we offer four counterpoints to the ones just stated.

Relativism is self-refuting. Remember the cartoons in which a character such as Wile E. Coyote is sitting on a tree limb and saws off that very limb by mistake? That's a good picture of a self-refuting position. A self-refuting position makes a claim that, oddly enough, must be false if the claim is true! Consider these examples:

"I CANNOT UTTER A SINGLE SENTENCE IN ENGLISH."

Oops! The speaker just did so.

"EVERY SENTENCE HAS ONLY FIVE WORDS."

One, two, three . . . hmmm.

"EVERYTHING I TELL YOU IS A LIE."

But is that statement itself a lie? This one's famous; it's a version of the Liar's Paradox. It's so brain-twisting that the logic-wielding Mister Spock used it in an episode of *Star Trek* ("I, Mudd") to overload the circuits on some androids.

OK, those were easy enough. But how about this one:

"NO IDEA IS TRUE FOR EVERYONE, BECAUSE ALL IDEAS
EXPRESS A POLITICAL VIEWPOINT."

If that's true, then the idea that all ideas express a political viewpoint
itself expresses a political viewpoint. But *that* idea is then, according to
the position stated, not true for everyone. But if it is not true that "no
idea is true for everyone," then some ideas *are* true for everyone! In
short, the above statement, when turned on itself, negates its own claim.
Relativistic statements in the end are all variations on the Liar's Paradox.
They are all statements to the effect that everything that is said is something other than the truth.

And what about this one?

"ANYONE WHO BELIEVES THAT HE IS RIGHT AND OTHERS
ARE WRONG IS INTOLERANT."

Here the speaker assumes that he is right in believing that people
are intolerant and bigoted if they believe that they are right and others
are wrong. His statement obviously implies that anyone who disagrees
with him is wrong (that is, it assumes that being intolerant is wrong).
Thus, the statement above expresses a self-refuting position. If no one
should criticize anyone else's beliefs, this includes the beliefs of those
people who think they're right and others are wrong.

It is, of course, true that people's beliefs are often tied to political interests. Postmodernists are right about that. Indeed, in making that observation, the postmodernist is uttering a truth about the real world. But the ability to recognize such political factors in beliefs is itself proof that we can know some things in a way that rises above narrow political interests. To say otherwise would be to negate the very truth the post-modernist recognizes.

Some facts are undeniable. Postmodernism gets a lot of mileage out of the diversity of opinions on just about every subject, from what God (if He exists) is like to who killed JFK. Our inability to arrive at consensus on such questions feeds our collective suspicion that ultimate truth is elusive if not illusory. But it is a colossal mistake to jump to the conclusion that we can't be certain about anything. The postmodernist argument can't even get off the ground without acknowledging some facts. That there is a wide variety of beliefs about God is a fact. That JFK is dead is a fact. Moreover, all or nearly all of us know that these are facts. There are, then, some facts that all people can (and should!) know that can serve as points of reference in discussions about truth.

> SOME BELIEFS ARE FALSE, AND WE KNOW THEM
> TO BE FALSE. SO IT DOES NO GOOD TO PUT A
> HALO ON THE NOTION OF TOLERANCE AS IF
> EVERYTHING COULD BE EQUALLY TRUE.
>
> —RAVI ZACHARIAS[2]

Love tolerates people *but tells them the* truth. Tolerance is an important value for human society, but we would insist that there is no need to sacrifice truth on the altar of tolerance. Think about it this way: Can the values of tolerating people and loving them ever conflict? Can you love someone and not tolerate them? Surely not—and if you could, we would surely choose love over tolerance. But love tells people the truth. If you love someone and you see that the person you love is about to do something dangerous—say, drive while drunk—the loving thing for you to do is to tell that person the truth: "You're drunk, and you shouldn't drive." (And you should give that person a ride home.) Tolerating people does not mean being indifferent to what they think or how they live. Tolerating people means not interfering with their right to think as they choose.

Today many people are afraid they will appear arrogant if they claim that their beliefs are actually true and not just something they find helpful or comforting. But there is nothing arrogant about claiming that one's beliefs are true. Of course, some people can express that claim in an arrogant *fashion*, but that is a different matter. In fact, some people express their skepticism or relativism in an arrogant fashion and put down people who don't accept those beliefs! The liberal postmodernist can be just as narrow-minded and arrogant as the most conservative fundamentalist.

On the other hand, some of the most respected persons of our time have made bold truth claims while retaining their reputations as humble, gracious persons. Consider two of the most famous and beloved women of the late twentieth century, Mother Theresa and Princess Diana. Was Mother Theresa arrogant when she spoke out against abortion in front of President Bill Clinton? Surely even most advocates of abortion rights would hesitate to accuse Mother Theresa of arrogance. Her decades of selfless service to the poor gave her "moral capital" that allowed her to speak her mind on a very controversial subject without losing respect in the eyes of most people who disagree with her.

Was Princess Diana arrogant when she spoke out against the use of land mines? It's hard to imagine anyone suggesting that she was arrogant for taking that stand. Yet the principle is the same—she not only held to a particular belief but also dared to say that she was *right* and that others should agree with her.

There is, then, nothing intolerant or arrogant about believing and even proclaiming that one's beliefs are the truth. Some people are indeed intolerant and arrogant, but those are failings in the persons, not in the beliefs. Sometimes, in fact, the arrogant person is right in what he says, even though he is wrong in the way that he says it.

Absolute truth presupposes some absolute reality. The problem with modernism is not, as postmodernists think, that it is looking for absolute truth (that is, truth that is truth for all people). The problem is that modernism undermines the very possibility of absolute truth by trying to anchor it in human reason. Ever since Immanuel Kant, the German Enlightenment philosopher, modernists have held that human beings do not discover knowledge, they *create* it—by imposing the rational categories of their own minds on the world. It was a short step from this modernist claim to the postmodernist claim that each community of human beings, and in the end each human being individually, imposes a distinct point of view on the world. In this respect, postmodernism is not liberated from modernism at all but is instead a more radical form of modernism. In short, the modernist and postmodernist agree that human beings create knowledge, but that assumption in the end destroys the very possibility of knowing absolute truth.

Could the modernist and postmodernist be right? Is knowledge merely a human construct? We would urge that this claim simply cannot be sustained for at least three reasons.

First, there is absolute truth that we can and do know (such as that $2 + 2 = 4$ or that human beings require water to live). We are not imposing human fictions on reality when we say these things; rather, we are *recognizing* truths that would be true even if for some odd reason we did not recognize them. Therefore, it cannot be true that human beings create knowledge.

Second—and this will be a familiar point—the claim that all human knowledge is created or imposed by the human mind is self-defeating. If John claims that all human knowledge is created by people's minds, John is claiming to know this. But then *this* knowledge of his would *also* have to be merely the construct of his mind—in which case, it is not really the case that human knowledge is a mere human construct. (Sorry if this is starting to make your head hurt!)

Third, despite what skeptical philosophers have said, and despite what many common people repeat when confronted with truth-claims that make them uncomfortable, knowledge of reality is something we all have and make use of every day. Regardless of your personal philosophy, when you cross a busy intersection, you usually look both ways to make sure there aren't large trucks moving quickly in your direction. In defiance of the soft-headed notion that good and evil are mere human conventions, you feel righteous indignation when your fellow citizens are killed in an act of terrorism. In that moment you just *know* that indiscriminately killing innocent men, women, and children is wrong. We may play games with our own heads sometimes, but the fact is that we do know some things incorrigibly—and much that we do not know we can learn.

If human beings do not create knowledge, what is its ultimate origin? We would suggest that ultimately human knowledge originates from the creation and design of God. The modernist is right in thinking that our minds are capable of knowing truth, but they cannot explain why our mental faculties and categories of thought should correspond to the real world. The answer that Christianity gives to this question is disarmingly simple: God designed our minds that way. God made the world, He made us, and He designed our minds to have the capacity to know and understand truth about the world in which He has placed us.

It turns out, then, that our ability to know truth is itself a kind of evidence for the existence of God. Admittedly, though, this doesn't tell us very much. If there is a God, some ideas about God will be true and others false. And if there is a God and He cares about us, it's reasonable to assume that He would make it possible for us to know He is there and to know what He expects of us. As we'll see, God has gone out of His way to do just that.

FOR FURTHER READING

Copan, Paul. *"True for You, But Not for Me": Deflating the Slogans that Leave Christians Speechless.* Minneapolis: Bethany House, 1998. "That's true for you, but not for me." "Who are you to judge others?" "Christians are so intolerant." Have you ever said or thought these things or wondered if these statements were right? Copan considers these and similar statements and explains why Christians need not be intolerant or bigoted when they affirm that God is real and that He has revealed himself in Jesus Christ.

Sire, James W. *Why Should Anyone Believe Anything at All?* Downers Grove, Ill.: InterVarsity, 1994. An intelligent, insightful book, discussing the question posed in the title.

3

THE EVIDENCE OF EXISTENCE

THE MOST ELEMENTARY QUESTION:
WHY IS THERE SOMETHING
RATHER THAN NOTHING?

God ... calls into being that which does not exist.
—PAUL (ROMANS 4:17 NASB)

We begin with a thought experiment—one that you may have already tried in the past. Try to imagine that there is nothing—no people, no planets, no stars, no universe, no angels, no God—absolutely nothing. Depending upon your temperament and experience, imagining absolute nothingness may be very difficult, perhaps even painful.

Obviously, absolute nothingness is not the case. Something exists. But it is equally obvious, at least to most people, that things could have been very different. As hard as it is to imagine, you might not even have existed. If your biological parents had not come together where they did, or if conception had not taken place when it did, you wouldn't be here—and arguably you might never have existed at all. Had that been the case, as much of a loss as that would have been, the human race and the universe would have carried on without you. Painful though the thought may be, we can imagine a world in which we were never born, like George Bailey in Frank Capra's whimsical film *It's a Wonderful Life.*

By the same token, we can imagine a universe in which the human race did not exist. We may feel that the universe would be immeasurably poorer without us, but there seems to be no good reason to think that the universe couldn't get along without our species. Perhaps the Earth could have been populated with the same myriads of plants and animals but without mankind. Or perhaps the universe could have existed as a lifeless place. All in all, a universe without life seems a dull alternative scenario but not one that is impossible or irrational.

What about the universe itself? Granted, it's here, but could things have been different? This is much more difficult to decide via a simple thought experiment. Most of us probably have no trouble imagining that the universe might have been a very different kind of universe—say, one in which there is no gravitational force or in which educators make millions of dollars while basketball players make minimum wage. But we're not sure if such alternate universes would work. What's really difficult to imagine, at least for some of us, is no universe existing at all. It can be easy to suppose that the universe just *is*. But is that right?

One of the most famous questions in human history is also one of the most basic: Why is there something rather than nothing? Our interest in this question is not academic. We want to know why the something *that includes us* exists. The question "Why is there something rather than nothing?" is simply a more general, all-encompassing version of the question "Why are we here?"

There are three basic answers to this question. (1) This big something that includes us has always existed for no reason; it just is. (2) This big something that includes us is one big spiritual It; we're all God or part of God. (3) This big something that includes us was brought into existence by Someone whose existence explains itself—namely, God.

Which of these answers is right?

ATHEISM: NO GOD AT ALL

> ## THE COSMOS IS ALL THERE IS, ALL THERE WAS, AND ALL THERE EVER WILL BE.
> —CARL SAGAN[1]

We begin with the least popular, though highly influential, answer: that the big something that includes us has always existed for no reason. In this view, asking why there is something rather than nothing is really asking a nonsense question. Why does the universe exist? It just does!

The technical name for this answer is *atheism*. Atheism is one of several comprehensive beliefs about reality that are called *worldviews*.[2] A worldview is just what it sounds like—a view of the world as a whole. Everyone has a worldview, whether they realize it or not. Well, *almost* everyone. Anyone who can think about the world as a whole can and does have some sort of worldview, even if it's not very well developed. Presumably, one-week-old infants do not have a worldview; and as far as we know, dogs and cats don't have worldviews. But if you can read this book, it's a safe bet that *you* have a worldview. The question is whether your worldview fits the world in which we all live.

> ## THE MOST PRACTICAL AND IMPORTANT THING ABOUT A MAN IS STILL HIS VIEW OF THE UNIVERSE.
> —G. K. CHESTERTON[3]

Looked at in one way, atheism is the simplest worldview. Atheism says that the world exists and nothing else—end of discussion. No God of any kind made the world or lives in or through the world. What you see is what you get. No doubt, for some people, this way of looking at the "big picture" seems straightforward and even obvious. They wonder why even introduce God into the picture.

> ## IF ATHEISM IS CORRECT, MAN IS ALONE. THERE IS NO GOD TO THINK FOR HIM, TO WATCH OUT FOR HIM, TO GUARANTEE HIS HAPPINESS. THESE ARE THE SOLE RESPONSIBILITY OF MAN.
> —GEORGE H. SMITH[4]

If indeed the world is self-explanatory—if its being here and its being what it is can be *best* explained without recourse to any divine power or being—then atheists would have a point. However, there are certain features of the world that make it difficult to view the world as self-explanatory. We'll mention four of these briefly.

First, the world has not always existed. The scientific evidence has now convinced the vast majority of research scientists studying the question that the universe has not always existed—that it had a beginning and has existed for a finite length of time. Many scientists have come to this conclusion reluctantly; they realize that if the universe had a beginning, a reasonable and perhaps unavoidable inference is that it has a Beginner.

Second, the world seems to have been "fixed" to make life possible. During the past forty years or so, scientists have discovered numerous factors in the structure and nature of the universe, of the solar system, and of the Earth that are just what they need to be for biological life to exist. Many of these factors have a very narrow range within which life would be even possible. In short, it would seem very unlikely that the universe just "happened" by chance to be hospitable to life; it seems more likely that the universe was designed as a home for biological life.

Third, biological life itself bears the marks of intelligent design. The complex order of life is of such a kind that its having originated without any purposeful intent guiding its origin seems very unlikely. The problem is compounded when one considers the nature of human beings.

Fourth, the world is a place in which some things are right or good and some things are not. That is, there is a moral order to the world. It is difficult if not impossible to explain why this is so if one assumes an atheistic, materialistic view of the world.

We will have more to say about these aspects of the world in the next several chapters. Our point here is this: A worldview needs to be able to account for all of these aspects or features of existence. The problem isn't merely that there is something rather than nothing; the problem is that the something that exists doesn't look self-explanatory.

PANTHEISM: GOD IS ALL

WE ARE ALL PART OF GOD. WE ARE ALL INDIVIDUALIZED REFLECTIONS OF THE GOD SOURCE. GOD IS US, AND WE ARE GOD.

—SHIRLEY MacLAINE[5]

Let's consider a second popular answer to the question of why there is something rather than nothing. This answer agrees with atheism that the big something that includes us just exists for no reason outside itself. However, it disagrees with the atheistic assumption that the world is ultimately the material, physical universe that we can see and feel. Instead, this second answer says that the world's existence is self-explanatory because the world is ultimately a manifestation or expression of infinite Spirit or Mind or Power. In other words, according to this answer, the world is in some sense to be identified as or with God.

The technical name for this worldview is *pantheism* (meaning the belief that all is God). Pantheism comes in a wide variety of flavors; we will consider the three most representative types of pantheism.

According to one popular form of pantheism, God alone exists and everything we think we see, feel, or experience (including our own personal identity) is an illusion. In our estimation, a perfectly sensible and telling objection to this form of pantheism is to respond, "That's funny—I don't feel like an illusion!" Our awareness of our own concrete, personal identities is simply too strong for most of us even to entertain the notion that we don't exist. Even if we were able to entertain the idea, anyone who did would inevitably engage in a kind of inner debate about whether he or she could possibly be a mere illusion—raising the question, if the person struggling with the question does not exist, who or what is debating the question?

A second form of pantheism solves the problem we just considered, but in doing so it creates an even bigger problem. According to this second variety of pantheism, God alone exists, therefore we are all God. The obvious objection to this form of pantheism is to respond, "That's funny—I don't remember being God!" If we were God, wouldn't we all know it?

> IF OUR MINDS ARE PART OF GOD, AND GOD IS NECESSARILY PERFECT, IT IS NECESSARILY THE CASE THAT MISTAKES ARE IMPOSSIBLE. BUT WE DO MAKE MISTAKES.
> —FRANCIS J. BECKWITH[*]

The third form of pantheism abandons the strict pantheistic claim that God alone exists. It contends that God and the world are distinct aspects of the totality of all reality. This idea is so different from the other forms of pantheism that it has its own name: *panentheism*. The *en* in the middle of the word stands for "in," so the word means the belief that God is *in* all. (Arguably, then, panentheism really is not a form of pantheism but is a different worldview.) A popular illustration used to explain panentheism likens God to the human soul and the world to the human body. God is thought of as the soul of the world—the life force or power that energizes the universe, makes the origin and sustenance of life possible, and gives us our moral order.

Panentheism has a lot more going for it, intellectually speaking, than the two forms of strict pantheism we considered. It doesn't put itself in the awkward position of having to claim either that we are all God but forgot or that we don't really exist. Also, unlike atheism, it recognizes that the world has features that are difficult to explain on the basis of physical forces inherent in matter. Not surprisingly, a good number of philosophers and religious thinkers have moved toward a panentheistic worldview.

The main difficulty with panentheism can be simply illustrated using the panentheists' own metaphor of God's relationship to the world being like that of the soul to the body. In a human being, the soul and body are mutually dependent upon one another; neither is complete without the other. (One may be able to *exist* without the other, but such a state of affairs is not normal or healthy; in fact, it's called *death!*) The obvious question is whether God is dependent upon the world in the same way that the soul is dependent upon the body. Does God need the world in order to live or in order to be complete and whole?

As we discuss more specific evidences for God's existence, we will see that this evidence is not best explained using the panentheist worldview. The best explanation is the existence of a God on whom the world utterly depends but who is self-sufficient and not dependent upon the world for His life or completeness. This leads us to the third major explanation for our existence.

THEISM: GOD MADE ALL

> AMAZING AS IT MAY SEEM, THE MOST PLAUSIBLE ANSWER TO THE QUESTION OF WHY SOMETHING EXISTS RATHER THAN NOTHING IS THAT GOD EXISTS.
> —WILLIAM LANE CRAIG[7]

The traditional answer to the question "Why is there something rather than nothing?" offered in the religions of Judaism, Islam, and Christianity is that God made something that was other than himself. This worldview is called *monotheism* (which means the belief in one God) or, more simply, *theism*. According to theism, all existence is divided into two categories: God and everything else. God's existence is self-explanatory, since God is eternal—without beginning or cause of any sort. This God chose to bring into existence everything else. God created the space/time universe and everything in it.

We can argue about whether the act of a Creator God is the only logically possible explanation for our being here, but it's hard to deny that this is a simple and reasonable explanation. As we have already suggested and will explain in greater depth shortly, this world has characteristics that strongly indicate that the world is not self-explanatory. Why is there something—a something that includes us—rather than nothing? The theist's answer is that Someone who has always existed, whose existence is in no sense dependent upon anyone or anything else, brought everything else into existence. This Someone is commonly called God.

We should point out that theism did not originate as a clever answer to the question of why something rather than nothing exists. Christians don't claim to have thought about the problem of existence deeply on our own and then one day said, "Hey! I bet God did all this!" Our report is this: God has introduced himself into the picture by revealing himself through the patriarchs, prophets, and apostles of the Bible, and especially in Jesus. If you will, God has come to us and said, "Hey! You see all this? I did that!" But then, having heard this message, we have thought about it and realized that God's existence is the best explanation for ours.

> IT REMAINS PASSING STRANGE THAT THERE EXISTS ANYTHING AT ALL. BUT IF THERE IS TO EXIST ANYTHING, IT IS FAR MORE LIKELY TO BE SOMETHING WITH THE SIMPLICITY OF GOD THAN SOMETHING LIKE THE UNIVERSE WITH ALL ITS CHARACTERISTICS CRYING OUT FOR EXPLANATION WITHOUT THERE BEING GOD TO EXPLAIN IT.
>
> —RICHARD SWINBURNE[8]

FOR FURTHER READING

Geisler, Norman L., and William D. Watkins. *Worlds Apart: A Handbook on World Views.* 2nd ed. Grand Rapids: Baker, 1989. An easy-to-follow introduction to the major worldviews, highlighting both the strengths and the weaknesses of each.

Sire, James W. *The Universe Next Door: A Basic Worldview Catalog.* 3rd ed. Downers Grove, Ill.: InterVarsity, 1997. A popular treatment of worldviews, written especially with college students in mind but of broader appeal.

4

The Evidence of the Universe's Beginning

THE UNIVERSE HASN'T ALWAYS
BEEN HERE, AND IT'S A GOOD
THING TOO.

*In the beginning God created
the heavens and the earth.*

—Genesis 1:1

In the preceding chapters, we have considered general evidences in

support of taking the idea of God seriously. We have pointed out that

there is truth, that we can know it, and that we cannot avoid having

some view or other about God and the world. Along the way we have

given hints of some of the evidence for believing in God.

It's now time to get into the nitty-gritty of the matter. If God exists, we ought to be able to point to specific evidences showing that He exists. And, in fact, we can. We begin with a piece of evidence that turned a great many minds in the twentieth century, if reluctantly, to acknowledge the existence of God: the evidence for the beginning of the universe.

FROM PHILOSOPHY TO SCIENCE

It used to be a matter of rarified abstract speculation whether or not our universe has always existed. Medieval philosophers debated whether it was possible to prove that the universe had a beginning. The twelfth-century Christian philosopher and theologian Thomas Aquinas maintained that there were plausible arguments on both sides of the question. He concluded that Christians should believe that the universe had a beginning because it was revealed in the Bible, although no persuasive philosophical argument could be constructed in support.

Western thinkers generally assumed that the universe had a beginning until the eighteenth and nineteenth centuries. In the late

eighteenth century, the influential German Enlightenment philosopher Immanuel Kant argued that the universe was infinite in size and
infinitely old. Modern philosophers and scientists quickly became
enthusiastic over the concept of an infinite universe, since it seemed
that in an infinite universe anything was possible. As telescopes got
bigger, the universe that we could see got bigger, too, seemingly confirming the theory that the universe was infinite in size. By the end of
the nineteenth century, the infinitude of the universe was widely
regarded almost as an axiom of science.

Then came the discoveries of twentieth-century science. Whoops!

SCIENCE RUNS INTO GOD

Albert Einstein started the ball rolling when he published his theory
of general relativity in 1917. Most people associate the theory of relativity with time travel and other science-fiction notions, but it's a *little* less
exotic than all that. What few people know is the use that was made of
Einstein's theories in the study of the origins of the universe. Shortly
after Einstein published his theory, the Dutch astronomer Willem de

Sitter studied Einstein's equations and derived from them the conclusion that the universe was expanding.

The math by itself was one thing; seeing it was another. Already in 1913, astronomers had noticed that several galaxies were moving away from us at high speeds. Later, Edwin Hubble used his hundred-inch telescope to verify de Sitter's mathematical prediction that "the farther away a galaxy is, the faster it moves"—implying that the universe was expanding from a central point of origin like an inflating balloon or like an explosion. At the same time, Hubble found that "nearby" galaxies were actually millions of light years away.[1] The implication of these findings was disturbingly obvious: the universe had a beginning. Specifically, it looked as though the universe had begun with an incredible explosion of matter and energy from an initial point of origin, generating intense light and heat that eventually diffused and cooled enough to allow for the formation of stars and planets.

The discovery that the universe had a beginning was not met with pleasure. Many scientists rebelled against the notion because it implied a Beginner. In fact, "Einstein was the first to complain."[2] At first he refused to believe that the universe was expanding and sought to find some mathematical way out of the conclusion that the universe had a beginning. Arthur Eddington, a scientist who had helped prove that the universe was expanding, admitted that he found the idea of a beginning "repugnant" and hoped that a "loophole" could be found to avoid the cosmic implication of a supernatural Creator. Hubble himself spent the rest of his life arguing against the theory his findings had helped to prove. With disdain, Fred Hoyle, another critic of the theory, labeled it the big bang.

During the middle third of the twentieth century, astronomers uncomfortable with the notion of a Creator tried out several "loopholes," floating a number of alternate explanations of the astronomical evidence. The two most popular were the steady-state theory, according to which the universe was merely expanding in some places but not in others; and the oscillating-universe theory, according to which the universe expands for many billions of years, then contracts back to a central point, explodes and expands again, and so on, ad infinitum. Both theories were developed specifically to avoid the specter of a finite universe that had a beginning.

In 1965 the steady-state theory was dealt a fatal blow, and the oscillating-universe theory was sent into critical condition. In that year Bell Telephone scientists Arno Penzias and Robert Wilson reported their discovery of the background radiation that the big bang hypothesis had predicted would be left behind by the initial explosion of the universe. Now, it seemed, the only hope for avoiding a creation was to show that the universe might be oscillating through an endless series of "big bangs."

The oscillating-universe theory suffered several setbacks over the years but none so devastating as the findings of the Cosmic Background Explorer (COBE) satellite, designed specifically to measure that background radiation more precisely than is possible from within Earth's atmosphere. In 1990 the COBE delivered its first findings: the radiation was so even throughout space that the universe must have begun with an extremely hot explosion from a central point of origin—too hot to be one in an endless series of explosions. In 1992 the COBE satellite yielded what Stephen Hawking, the famous author of *A Brief History of Time,* called "the discovery of the century, if not of all time."[3] The COBE revealed that the background radiation, though extremely even, had just enough irregularities (of an extremely minute amount) to account for the formation of the "clumps" of hot matter that formed into our universe's galaxies.[4]

These discoveries led to the almost complete triumph in modern cosmology of the big bang theory. This isn't to say that all scientists now believe in the personal Creator God of the Bible; many still fiercely resist that understanding of God. But scientists now have to admit that the evidence for the universe's beginning at least implies the existence of some kind of God. Even Stephen Hawking, who dislikes the notion of a personal God involved in His creation, credits the existence of the universe to "the mind of God."[5]

Moreover, the fact that the universe had a beginning is most naturally and simply explained if theism, rather than pantheism, is the correct view of God. In theism, God is understood as a distinct, eternal being who brought the universe into existence by an act of His will. All three of the major theistic religions—Judaism, Christianity, and Islam—historically have maintained that the universe has not always existed. It turns out they were right all along.

Pantheism, on the other hand, has historically viewed the universe as a manifestation of the divine All. For that reason, pantheists have often viewed the universe as eternal or believed in an endless, eternal cycle of universes. (When the oscillating-universe theory was taken seriously, one of the reasons for its popularity among some scientists was that it supported pantheism over theism.) It now looks as though that view was incorrect.

The beginning of the universe, then, is a significant piece of evidence supporting the biblical message that God created the world.

> FOR THE SCIENTIST WHO HAS LIVED BY HIS FAITH IN THE POWER OF REASON, THE STORY ENDS LIKE A BAD DREAM. HE HAS SCALED THE MOUNTAINS OF IGNORANCE; HE IS ABOUT TO CONQUER THE HIGHEST PEAK; AS HE PULLS HIMSELF OVER THE FINAL ROCK, HE IS GREETED BY A BAND OF THEOLOGIANS WHO HAVE BEEN SITTING THERE FOR CENTURIES.
>
> —ROBERT JASTROW[6]

WE'VE GOT BAD NEWS AND GOOD NEWS...

Many people don't like the idea that the universe had a beginning and therefore has not always been here. But it turns out that it's a very good thing that the universe is not infinitely old. A universe that was infinitely old, or even extremely old compared to its present age (say, a trillion years old), would not be a nice place to live or even to visit.

The reason is not hard to see, although it is hard to look at directly: the sun. Our sun is just one of the hundreds of billions of stars in the universe. In the twentieth century, astronomers came to understand some-thing very clearly about the sun. (You might want to sit down; it's not particularly good news.) *The sun will eventually die.* The sun is, essen-tially, a big fireball, burning away at the center of our solar system. It's an extremely large fireball, of course, but, like all fires, it will eventually burn itself out. Scientists consider the sun to be a middle-aged star; it's been burning for several billion years, and several billion years from now, if all goes as expected, it will burn itself out.

Bummer, you say? Well, it is a bit unsettling to learn that our source of light and heat won't last forever. But think about it from the other direction. If the sun will eventually burn itself out, that means the sun hasn't always been here. The same is true of the universe as a whole. If the universe were infinitely old, our sun would have gone through its "life cycle" and died by now. You see, the universe won't be able to keep forming new stars forever. There's only so much hydrogen to go around. As the universe continues to expand, its energy is being gradu-ally diffused. The universe itself started out as a kind of fireball, and eventually—unless God supernaturally intervenes—the universe will fizzle out.

That may sound like even worse news, but surprisingly, this cloud has a silver lining. It turns out that biological life would be nigh impossible on a planet orbiting anything but a middle-aged star. A bright young star would be too hot for us to handle, and a quiet, mature star would leave us cold. Our sun, though rather boring as stars go, is just what we need.

It turns out that there are a lot of things about our universe, solar system, and Earth that are just right. We'll talk about these things and their implications for God's existence in the next chapter.

For Further Reading

Jastrow, Robert. *God and the Astronomers.* New York: Norton, 1978. An agnostic and professional astronomer tells the story of the triumph of the big bang theory and its religious implications over the resistance of scientists.

Ross, Hugh. *The Creator and the Cosmos: How the Greatest Scientific Discoveries of the Century Reveal God.* 2nd ed. Colorado Springs: NavPress, 1999. A Christian astronomer details the discoveries of the last decade of the twentieth century and explains how they support belief in the God of the Bible.

5
THE EVIDENCE OF THE UNIVERSE'S FITNESS FOR LIFE

> SOMEBODY WENT TO A LOT OF
> TROUBLE TO MAKE IT POSSIBLE FOR
> US TO BE HERE.

Two of the most popular *Star Trek* films have as their premise the invention of a device that can in very short order transform a dead planet into an Earth-like world teeming with life. "Project Genesis," as it was called, was meant to solve the growing Federation's population problem: too many people, not enough habitable planets. In *Star Trek II: The Wrath of Khan*, the device is detonated, creating the Genesis planet, which is quickly covered in lush vegetation.

In *Star Trek III: The Search for Spock*, the crew of the *Enterprise* learns that this artificial Genesis does not quite live up to its name. The scientist who developed the Genesis device used an unstable element that ethical Federation scientists had condemned. In a very short time, the planet's core destabilizes, the surface is ravaged by volcanic eruptions, and the paradisiacal environment of the planet is destroyed. As Spock had commented, "As a matter of cosmic history, it has always been easier to destroy than to create."[1]

Even in the twenty-third century, it's hard to make a decent planet.

Where were you when I laid
the foundation of the earth?
—GOD, SPEAKING TO JOB (JOB 38:4)

WAS THE BIG BANG AN ACCIDENT?

In the preceding chapter, we talked about the scientific evidence that the universe had a beginning in what is commonly called the big bang. We explained that if the universe had a beginning, one reasonable explanation for that beginning is that it had a Beginner.

Some people, however, find the idea of God starting the universe off with a "bang" to be strange. The expression "big bang" sounds like the universe began with a violent, destructive accident. Unfortunately, in this regard the nickname "big bang" (which Fred Hoyle, an opponent of the theory, had given to it) turns out to be a misnomer of literally cosmic proportions. Far from a haphazard, destructive event, the big bang was the initial event in which the universe came into existence with all of its physical laws, its energy and matter, and its processes.

In the last forty years or so, scientists have been engaged in one of the most fascinating research projects in the history of humanity. They have been studying the parameters of our physical world that have made life possible. What they have discovered is that everything in the universe seems to have been extremely "fine-tuned" to make life possible. In this chapter, we will review just a little of this evidence and then explain why this evidence supports belief in God.

A "Just Right" Universe

A variety of factors or parameters for the entire universe were set in place essentially at the initial moment, or within an extremely small fraction of the first second, of the beginning of the universe. It turns out that these parameters had to be what they are, to within a very narrow margin, in order for any sort of life to exist.

Fundamental forces: the right stuff. There are four fundamental forces (that we know of) that are constant throughout the universe and that affect all physical objects everywhere. The *strong nuclear force* is the force that binds subatomic particles (such as neutrons and protons) together within the nuclei of atoms. If this force were stronger or weaker by more than about 1 percent, the universe would be either all hydrogen or have no hydrogen at all. All hydrogen or no hydrogen at all would make the universe a very dull place.

The *weak nuclear force* makes radioactive decay, fission, and fusion possible. If this force had been a bit stronger or weaker, the universe would have produced far too little or far too much helium in its early history; either way, you could forget about having any planets.

The *electromagnetic force* binds electrons to the nuclei of atoms. If this force were slightly weaker, the electrons would fly away—and so would any chance for molecules. If the electromagnetic force were slightly stronger, atoms could not "share" electrons—and again, no molecules. Not an attractive outlook for life.

The *gravitational force*—the easiest one to notice—is also just right. If it were somewhat stronger, the stars would be so hot that they would burn out too quickly and unevenly; the planets near them might make interesting places to visit, but you couldn't live there. If gravity were somewhat weaker, the stars would not become hot enough to ignite nuclear fusion. Such stars would burn quietly for a long time but make no heavy elements needed for planets, leaving us no place to visit, let alone live.

All of these forces work at just the right strength to make our universe the interesting place that it is. As Stephen Hawking observed, "The remarkable fact is that the values of these numbers seem to have been very finely adjusted to make possible the development of life."[2]

A most excellent bang. In order for the universe to be at all hospitable for life—*anywhere*—it isn't enough that the universe get fired up and start expanding. Let's just mention two things that happen to be just right about the big bang. If the *expansion rate* of the universe were just a tad faster or slower, we wouldn't be here to think about it. That's because if the universe had expanded just a tiny bit more slowly, gravity would have slowed the expansion and caused the universe to cave back in on itself a long time ago in what cosmologists call a Big Crunch. On the other hand, if the universe were expanding just a wee bit faster, gravity would not have been able to attract material together into gases, galaxies, and the like. In other words, if the expansion rate and the gravitational force had not been very precisely balanced indeed, the universe would have been either very short-lived or very dull.

The other thing that's just right about the big bang is the smoothness or evenness of the "explosion," what scientists call its *isotropy.* Back in the 1980s, cosmologists figured out that if the universe did begin with a big bang, it would have needed to result in an almost, but not quite, perfectly isotropic distribution of matter and radiation. The COBE (Cosmic Background Explorer) satellite showed that the isotropy of the universe was just right, to within a practically infinitesimal degree. The Oxford mathematician Roger Penrose calculated the allowable margin of error as 1 in 10 to the 10^{123}—a number that is just too big to explain![3] Penrose commented that this is far more than the number of subatomic particles in the universe, but to be honest, we didn't count them to make sure.

THE MORE I STUDY NATURE, THE MORE
I AM AMAZED AT THE CREATOR.

—LOUIS PASTEUR

The point is that the universe seems to be perfectly, exquisitely set to just the right parameters for it to have even the *potential* to sustain life. It appears that the universe could have started out in a trillion or more different ways that would have failed to produce even a potential home for life. Yet, here we are.

A "JUST RIGHT" SOLAR SYSTEM

OK, you say, perhaps having a stable universe with stars and such is a wonderful bit of luck, but given that the universe is here, how surprising is it that it contains life? After all, the universe seems to be a very big place, and it's been around for an awfully long time.

Indeed, it is. The sheer size of the universe is especially breathtaking and difficult for us to fathom. Our own galaxy, the Milky Way, has over a hundred billion stars in it, and there are hundreds of billions of galaxies in the universe. The nearest star to us besides our own sun, Proxima Centauri, is about 24 trillion miles away. The nearest galaxy outside of our own, Andromeda, is some 18 million trillion miles away. It takes about four years for light to reach us from Proxima Centauri and about three *million* years for light to reach us from Andromeda.

To put all this into some limited perspective, imagine that our sun was the size of a ping-pong ball (which is roughly 50 billion times smaller than the actual size of the sun). The Earth, which would then be the size of a speck of dust about 1/100 of an inch across, orbits the sun some ten feet away. Pluto, the furthermost planet (of which we are aware), orbits about 120 yards out. Even on this greatly reduced scale, Proxima Centauri would be another ping-pong ball roughly 500 miles away from our "ping-pong" sun; and the Andromeda galaxy would be a collection of billions of ping-pong balls some 350 million miles away.

Given the existence of hundreds of billions of galaxies containing billions of stars each, it may seem that there are virtually endless possible places for life to flourish. But this impression is more of a feeling than anything else. As scientists have studied the parameters necessary for biological life to exist, they have discovered that the odds are surprisingly small that the universe just happens to include places where life can dwell.

First of all, not any old galaxy will do. Some galaxies are too close to one another or too close to another large galaxy so that the galaxies actually interfere gravitationally with each other. Some galaxies are too large and hot, making stable star systems virtually impossible. Galaxies that are too elliptical or too irregular also would have a difficult time sustaining a stable star system. (Our galaxy is a nicely organized spiral.) How many galaxies might be the right size and shape and in the right kind of location? No one's sure, but an estimate of one in every thousand is reasonable.

The right galaxy, of course, will have billions of stars. However, most of these stars are not suitable candidates for stable solar systems. The star must be in the right place and be the right kind of star. Take our Milky Way galaxy, for example. Stars in the central mass of stars, or deep within the spiral arms of the galaxy, will generally be too close together. Stars far from the spiral arms won't likely do well either, because such stars probably won't be able to produce enough heavy elements to make planets. (Our star is on the fringe of a spiral arm, not too close and not too far.) Most of the stars in the right parts of the galaxy, though, will not be the right kind of star. Most will be too big (and thus too hot and unstable) or too small. Moreover, binary stars—systems in which two stars are locked into orbit around each other—are very unlikely places to sustain planets where life could live. (That scene in the first *Star Wars* film in which Luke Skywalker watches two suns setting—

forget it! Very romantic but also very unscientific.) Perhaps only one in a billion stars is the right kind of star in the right kind of place.

If a good star is hard to find, a good solar system is even harder. Only in recent years have we begun to appreciate just how special our solar system is. First of all, of course, the system needs planets. Cosmologists debate how common planets are; a reasonable guess is that there might be an average of one planet per star. And one might suppose that one would be enough—that a good star just needs one planet for life to be possible. However, we now know this is not so.

For example, it turns out that having a planet about the size of Jupiter out beyond our planet Earth is vital to our survival. Jupiter's large gravity sucks away a large percentage of the asteroids and comets that might otherwise intersect with Earth's orbit. If Jupiter were smaller or further away, it would not perform that job well enough to protect Earth. On the other hand, if Jupiter were larger or closer, it would interfere with Earth's orbit.

Earth also benefits greatly from having a large moon. With all the planets in our solar system, Earth is the only one to have such a large moon. It turns out to be just the right size and distance away from the

Earth to help stabilize Earth's orbit and to produce tidal effects that are significant but not destructive.

Other things need to be just right in a life-friendly solar system, but you probably get the idea. Even among stars that are the right kind and in the right place, our solar system is probably one in a billion—and maybe much, much rarer than that.

A "Just Right" Earth

It's fascinating to consider that in the 1960s, about the same time as we were beginning to uncover evidence suggesting that our planet is likely to be a rather extraordinary place in the universe, we actually got to see it from a distance for the first time. The blue and white marble in space that we call home not only looks special, we have accumulated a large body of scientific evidence confirming that it really is special.

Location, location, location! The most basic requirement for a decent planet to support life is its location. Presumably, as one or more planets formed around a star, such planets could form at virtually any distance from that star (between the extremes of so close that it is pulled into the star or so far that it escapes the star's gravity). Yet the region around the star within which a planet must consistently orbit in order to sustain life, at least above the level of a microbe, is a very narrow band. For example, for our sun that band is a region roughly 90 to 100 million miles from the sun (and Earth happens to orbit about 93 million miles away). Go back to our illustration of the solar system reduced by a factor of 50 billion: the Earth orbits at about ten feet from the sun and Pluto, the outermost planet, at about 120 yards out. On this model, if the Earth were more than eleven or less than nine feet from the sun, life there would be impossible. Imagine dropping a few grains of fine sand randomly from a low-flying plane over a football field and needing one of them to land on the paint of the three-yard line at one end: that is about the accuracy needed.

Many other such factors have been discovered. The size and surface gravity of the planet (which of course are interrelated) must be just right. Too big and heavy, and the atmosphere will be rich with noxious elements like ammonia and methane; too small and light, and the atmosphere won't retain water. The planet must turn on its axis and be tilted just enough to prevent extremes of temperature and weather. The planet must be composed of various heavy elements to make complex molecules and compounds (such as water) possible. It must have a crust

THE EVIDENCE OF THE UNIVERSE'S FITNESS FOR LIFE

that's thick enough to keep volcanoes from dominating the surface and thin enough to allow the atmosphere to retain oxygen. Imagine a pizza restaurant needing to use sensitive equipment to ensure that their pizza crusts stayed between, say, 0.181 and 0.182 inches in thickness!

These are merely a few of the parameters that must be just right for a planet to sustain biological life of any kind. A fair, even generous estimate is that among all the planets that may exist in acceptable solar systems, probably no more than one in ten billion will be hospitable to life (at least above the microscopic level).

WHAT ARE THE ODDS?

Computing the probability that a planet capable of sustaining life might exist somewhere in the universe is not yet anything like an exact science. However, we have enough information to know that the probability is extremely low. The table below pulls together the rough estimates that we noted in our discussion to this point and derives a conclusion as to the probability of a life-friendly planet existing somewhere in this universe.

Right kind of galaxy	1 in a thousand (10^3) in the universe
Right kind of star	1 in a billion (10^9) in acceptable galaxies
Right kind of solar system	1 in a billion (10^9) in acceptable stars
Right kind of planet	1 in 10 billion (10^{10}) in acceptable solar systems
Right kind of planet	1 in 10 quadrillion quadrillion (10^{31}) in the universe (10^3 x 10^9 x 10^9 x 10^{10} = 10^{31})
Likely number of actual planets	10 billion trillion (10^{22}) in the universe
Probability of one good planet	1 in a billion (10^9) in the universe ($10^{31}/10^{22}$ = 10^9)

Keep in mind that this probability of one in a billion represents an extremely conservative estimate. Well over a hundred parameters of the types we have discussed here have been identified, and it is likely that more will be discovered. One astronomer has estimated the odds of a life-friendly planet existing anywhere in the universe by chance to be less than 1 in 10^{129}—that's one in one thousand quintillion quintillion quintillion quintillion quintillion quintillion quintillion![4] Such estimates are actually more representative of scientific opinion. As Steven Weinberg (a Nobel-Prize-winning astrophysicist) rather gloomily put it, our Earth "is just a tiny part of an overwhelmingly hostile universe."[5]

To review: It appears that, given that the universe began with something like the big bang, the likelihood that it would be a decent kind of universe where life might have a chance is something like one in a trillion (if not much, much less). Even with this very nice universe that we have, the probability that one of its planets would be capable of sustaining life would seem to be one in a billion, if not worse. Thus, the probability of the big bang producing a stable universe and then having a planet where life could safely thrive is no better than one in a billion trillion (and probably much worse).

And yet, here we are. How is this to be explained?

JUST LUCKY, I GUESS?

One popular response to the evidence of the fine-tuning of the universe, solar system, and Earth is that we got lucky. This is essentially the answer that all atheists must give to the question. In their book *Rare Earth,* Peter Ward and Donald Brownlee, scientists at the University of Washington in Seattle, appear to defend this interpretation:

> *If some god-like being could be given the opportunity to plan a sequence of events with the express goal of duplicating our "Garden of Eden," that power would face a formidable task. With the best intentions, but limited by natural laws and materials, it is unlikely that Earth could*

ever be truly replicated. Too many processes in its formation involved sheer luck.[6]

Ward and Brownlee never even discuss the idea that an actual *God*, rather than "some god-like being," was responsible.

To explain how we could have been so lucky, some thinkers have used the analogy of the lottery winner. In a typical state lottery, a player might pick five numbers between 1 and 50, a separate number between 1 and 50, and hope to match the random drawing exactly. The lottery winner is surprised that he won, because the probability was about one in a hundred million that he would win. But he really should not be surprised, we are told; after all, *someone* had to win.[7]

The problem with this analogy is that in a lottery, your chances of winning are extremely low only because the game was designed to be played by millions of people but won by only one or a few players. If you played the lottery one time, and no one else played, and you won, that would indeed be very surprising! In the game of "Life in the Universe," though, there could be no guarantee that the universe would include a place that could support life—unless someone designed the universe that way.

To circumvent objections such as the one just given, some atheists suggest that this universe might be merely one of many, many universes—perhaps millions or even an infinite number of universes. They admit that in virtually all universes, life will be impossible; we just happen to live in a universe where life is possible and actually exists. But *even if we knew* that other universes existed, this speculation wouldn't solve the problem at all.

Suppose you find a penny and begin flipping it over and over. To your surprise, it keeps coming up heads. After the hundredth toss yields yet another heads, you will begin suspecting that the coin has been weighted or "fixed" in some way. (Rightly so; the chances of getting heads a hundred times in a row are less than one in a quadrillion quadrillion!) It would make no sense to reason that since there are over a hundred billion pennies in circulation, one of them was bound to come up heads a hundred or more times in a row. Even if a quadrillion quadrillion pennies were in circulation, the best and most sensible explanation for getting heads a hundred times in a row would be that the coin was fixed. Likewise, the fact that the universe has an extraordinary combination of highly precise parameters and features, all of which are necessary for any life to be possible at all, cannot be explained by postulating the existence of a quadrillion other universes.

Of course, the other problem is that we don't know if any other universes exist or not. And if they did, we'd still have to explain what causes these universes to pop into existence with whatever physical laws and constants and material and features that they might have.

Admissions (Some Grudging) of Apparent Design

> THE ODDS AGAINST A UNIVERSE LIKE OURS EMERGING OUT OF SOMETHING LIKE THE BIG BANG ARE ENORMOUS.... I THINK CLEARLY THERE ARE RELIGIOUS IMPLICATIONS WHENEVER YOU START TO DISCUSS THE ORIGINS OF THE UNIVERSE.
>
> —Stephen W. Hawking[8]

> A COMMONSENSE INTERPRETATION OF THE FACTS SUGGESTS THAT A SUPER INTELLECT HAS MONKEYED WITH PHYSICS, AS WELL AS CHEMISTRY AND BIOLOGY, AND THAT THERE ARE NO BLIND FORCES WORTH SPEAKING ABOUT IN NATURE. THE NUMBERS ONE CALCULATES FROM THE FACTS SEEM TO ME SO OVERWHELMING AS TO PUT THIS CONCLUSION ALMOST BEYOND QUESTION.
>
> —Fred Hoyle[9]

PHYSICISTS ARE RUNNING INTO STONE
WALLS OF THINGS THAT SEEM TO REFLECT
INTELLIGENCE AT WORK IN NATURAL LAW.
—CHARLES TOWNES[10]

THE IMPRESSION OF DESIGN IS OVERWHELMING.
—PAUL DAVIES[11]

THE FINE TUNING OF THE UNIVERSE PROVIDES
PRIMA FACIE EVIDENCE OF DEISTIC DESIGN.
TAKE YOUR CHOICE: BLIND CHANCE THAT
REQUIRES MULTITUDES OF UNIVERSES
OR DESIGN THAT REQUIRES ONLY ONE.
—ED HARRISON[12]

HOW IS IT THAT COMMON ELEMENTS SUCH AS
CARBON, NITROGEN, AND OXYGEN HAPPENED TO
HAVE JUST THE KIND OF ATOMIC STRUCTURE THAT
THEY NEEDED TO MAKE THE MOLECULES UPON
WHICH LIFE DEPENDS? IT IS ALMOST AS THOUGH
THE UNIVERSE HAD BEEN CONSCIOUSLY DESIGNED.
—RICHARD MORRIS[13]

THE UNIVERSE, IT SEEMS, IS FINE-TUNED TO
LET LIFE AND CONSCIOUSNESS FLOWER.
—EDWARD KOLB[14]

THE MORE I EXAMINE THE UNIVERSE AND THE
DETAILS OF ITS ARCHITECTURE, THE MORE EVIDENCE
I FIND THAT THE UNIVERSE IN SOME SENSE MUST
HAVE KNOWN WE WERE COMING.

—FREEMAN DYSON[15]

SOMEONE FIXED THINGS!

By far the most popular answer, and one that is enjoying significant support from many scientists themselves, is that the universe was designed by a supreme intelligence to make it possible for life to exist here. The logic underlying this conclusion is not difficult to follow. That the universe is arranged in a highly specific fashion to make it possible for life to exist is entailed in the very concept of a Creator God. The evidence for this life-favoring arrangement is just the sort of findings one would expect if one believed in God.

The fact is that this world seems to have been engineered to make it possible for us to be here. If you don't like the idea of God, you can always call it luck, but that isn't much of an explanation. A personal and highly intelligent Creator—God, as He is commonly known—is by far the simplest and best explanation.

FOR FURTHER READING

Ross, Hugh. " Big Bang Model Refined by Fire." In *Mere Creation: Science, Faith & Intelligent Design,* ed. William A. Dembski, 363-84. Downers Grove, Ill.: InterVarsity Press, 1998. One of several writings in which Ross sets forth the evidence for the fine-tuning of the universe and of the Earth.

Swenson, Richard A., M.D. *More Than Meets the Eye: Fascinating Glimpses of God's Power and Design.* Colorado Springs: NavPress, 2000. A nicely-written popular presentation of the scientific evidence that God is behind the "coincidences" of the cosmos.

6

THE EVIDENCE OF LIFE'S ORIGIN

THE MORE WE LEARN ABOUT THE
ORIGIN OF LIFE, THE MORE OF A
PUZZLE IT BECOMES.

So far we have seen that the universe had a beginning and that everything about the universe and our own planet Earth seems to be very carefully arranged to make it possible for life to exist here. The biblical claim that God is responsible for the existence and order of the world enjoys a depth of support from the scientific evidence that is quite staggering. Admittedly, it may be possible to imagine scenarios in which all of these things have come about without the agency of a personal Creator. But it cannot reasonably be denied that the evidence is just what a believer in God would expect—and, as many scientists have testified, the evidence is just what an atheist would *not* expect. Our claim is that the existence of God is the best explanation for the evidence.

> You send forth Your Spirit, they are created;
> And You renew the face of the ground.
> —PSALM 104:30 NASB

In this chapter we will add to the evidence by looking at the origin of life. It is one thing to say that it is amazing that a place exists where life *could* flourish. But a nice environment is no guarantee that life will exist. The more scientists have learned about the origin of life on Earth, the more difficulties they have encountered explaining that origin as a natural, random event.

Fifty, even twenty-five years ago, many scientists were confident that the origin of life on Earth could be explained as the result of purely natural, unguided processes. The conventional scenario went like this: After the Earth cooled down from the heat of its initial formation, a long period of time (perhaps a billion or two billion years) passed before life emerged. During that period, the Earth's atmosphere was rich in heavy gases, particularly ammonia and methane, and very poor in oxygen. In this "primordial soup" environment, the first amino acids and then the first proteins formed spontaneously. One thing led to another, and after a few hundred million years or so, you've got cells multiplying like rabbits.

Never happened.[1]

The more we've learned during the past quarter-century about the early Earth, the more difficult the above naturalistic origin-of-life scenario has been to maintain. Naturalists have scrambled to come up with different versions of the story, but so far none is sticking.

READY, SET . . . LIFE!

Of the several problems facing all of the naturalistic explanations of the origin of life, we will mention just three. The first is that life appeared on Earth far too soon—almost four billion years ago, or roughly half a billion years after the Earth was first formed. Half a billion years sounds like a long time, but in actuality this leaves no significant amount of time for life to originate spontaneously after the Earth had reached a state where such life could survive for any length of time. As Ward and Brownlee point out, "As soon as the rain of asteroids ceased and surface temperatures on Earth permanently fell below the boiling point of water, life seems to have appeared."[2] In other words, "Life thus arose here almost as soon as it theoretically could."[3]

Imagine that your wife baked an apple pie and announced to the family as she took it out of the oven that it needed to cool for half an hour before it could be eaten. You go about your business and wait to be summoned for dessert. Thirty-two minutes later, you hear her demanding to know who took a piece of pie. You *could* surmise that one of the kids had not heard her and just happened upon the pie while walking through the kitchen and decided on an impulse to take a piece. However, you would almost certainly not draw such a conclusion. Rather, you would infer that the youngster deliberately waited until the half-hour had passed and then took a piece as soon as it was edible.

Likewise, one *could* choose to believe that life just happened to burst spontaneously into existence as soon as the Earth was cool enough to sustain it. However, the timing of the event is suspicious, to say the least. It's almost as if something—or Someone—was waiting for the Earth to be ready before getting life started here.

HEY, WE'RE NOT READY FOR THE OXYGEN JUST YET

A second major problem for the soup-to-cells story is that the Earth's atmosphere during the time that life first appeared had too much oxygen. That may sound strange—after all, most forms of life need oxygen to *survive*—but lots of oxygen would actually have interfered with the chemical reactions that would have been necessary to get the first life forms assembled. Oxygen forms compounds easily with many other atoms and compounds, a process known as *oxidizing*. The standard scenarios of a naturalistic origin of life have all assumed that the Earth's atmosphere was not oxidizing during the period when life originated.

The scientific evidence solidly shows, however, that the Earth has had an oxidizing atmosphere for about four billion years. The nonoxidizing atmosphere of life's primordial soup is essentially wishful thinking. Some literature that discusses the origin of life still states as a fact that the Earth's atmosphere at the time was not oxidizing—because it *must* have been in order for life to originate spontaneously and many scientists *assume* that it must. But the evidence from rocks dating to that period (four billion to three-and-a-half billion years ago) shows that the atmosphere was oxidizing then. You see, if there was a primordial "soup" conducive to the spontaneous formation of life, it should have left behind a residue in the rocks with lots of the organic compounds that are the building blocks of life. But that's not what geologists have found. Instead, they have found rocks dating from that period containing large quantities of oxidized iron—what we usually call *rust*. And that's exactly what they should not find if the standard soup-to-cells scenario were true.

> IT IS BECOMING CLEAR THAT HOWEVER LIFE BEGAN ON EARTH, THE USUALLY CONCEIVED NOTION THAT LIFE EMERGED FROM AN OCEANIC SOUP OF ORGANIC CHEMICALS IS A MOST IMPLAUSIBLE HYPOTHESIS. WE MAY THEREFORE WITH FAIRNESS CALL THIS SCENARIO "THE MYTH OF THE PREBIOTIC SOUP."
> —CHARLES B. THAXTON, WALTER L. BRADLEY, AND ROGER L. OLSEN[4]

To get around the problem of an oxidizing atmosphere, some scientists have thought up some very creative alternate scenarios for the origin of life. Of these, we will mention just one.[5] According to the theory of *panspermia,* life actually did not form on Earth originally but was seeded here by meteors, comets, or other debris from space.

Obviously, this theory admits that attempts to explain how life could have originated on Earth itself have failed. The one thing this theory has going for it also kills it: There is no doubt that the Earth was heavily bombarded with such objects and debris during the first billion years of its history (especially the first half-billion years). But many of the objects that struck the Earth during that period were so large that they would have destroyed any life that might have been thus temporarily transplanted here. For this and other reasons, most scientists today do not give much credence to the panspermia theory. (Notice, by the way, that this theory never accounts for the origin of the living "seeds"; it merely sidesteps this problem by pushing it back to an earlier locale.)

Can You Spell "Deoxyribonucleic"?

The third major problem for a naturalistic origin of life is that the evidence strongly points to a highly orchestrated, carefully planned set of operations. There are two basic reasons why this is so.

First, the basic components of life on the molecular level need to exist *simultaneously* for each to function properly. DNA (deoxyribonucleic

20 COMPELLING EVIDENCES THAT GOD EXISTS

acid), RNA (ribonucleic acid), and proteins need each other in order to do what they do. It's doubtful at best that one could get elemental bits of any one of these three components to originate in a "natural" occurrence; it's virtually certain that these three components could not have been generated spontaneously at the same time in the same place. Origin-of-life theorists, recognizing this to be the case, have been speculating since the late 1980s that a special "super" kind of RNA could have been generated first and today's RNA, DNA, and proteins all evolved naturally from that super RNA. At this point, though, the super-RNA theory seems to be little more than wishful thinking.[6]

The second reason that life's origin appears to have been planned is that each of the three major components we just mentioned is highly complex and specified—in such a way that no gradual process (or even sudden, natural event) is likely ever to explain. For example, amino acids can come in two basic kinds of molecules called left-handed and right-handed—but living things on Earth all use only left-handed amino acid molecules. Experiments intended to simulate the natural generation of amino acids produce both left-handed and right-handed molecules. Imagine dumping a hundred Scrabble tiles on the floor in the hope of randomly spelling out a long sentence or even a couple of short

90

words. Your first problem would be that roughly half of the tiles would be upside down.

> EINSTEIN SAID, "GOD DOES NOT PLAY DICE."
> HE WAS RIGHT. GOD PLAYS SCRABBLE.
> —PHILIP GOLD[7]

Even more striking, these molecules are arranged in living things in extremely complex ways that yield high levels of *information*—meaningful codes or instructions that make possible the operations of all life. Again, imagine that your Scrabble tiles have been dumped, and for the sake of argument we'll stipulate that they will all land faceup. You would not consider it a miracle if one or two sequences of adjacent tiles happened to spell very short, unrelated words:

	T	H	E						
			B						
			U						
			T						
					D	O	E	S	

It would be immediately considered an act of some unseen intelligence, however, if a large number of tiles were to form a nice crossword with both short and long words in which the words composed an intelligible sentence:

				N		I						
		A	B	O	U	T						
				B								
		D		O		A						
		O		D		B						
E	V	E	R	Y	B	O	D	Y				
		S				U						
						T	A	L	K	S		
						N						
		B	U	T		Y						
				H		T						
			W	E	A	T	H	E	R			
						I						
						N						
						G						

The basic building blocks of life are far more complex and information-rich than our little Scrabble crossword. Michael Denton, like many scientists, uses a similar analogy:

The linear sequence of amino acids in a protein can be thought of as a

sentence made up of a long combination of the twenty amino acid letters. Just as different sentences are made up of different sequences of letters, so different proteins are made up of different sequences of amino acids. In most proteins the amino acid chain is between one hundred and five hundred amino acids long.[8]

Another analogy that Denton uses compares a single living cell to a giant factory filled with machines. "DNA is only found in the nucleus of the cell, equivalent to the head office of the factory, and contains the master blueprints." RNA molecules are like photocopies of the master blueprints that are delivered to the factory floor, where the machines (proteins) are assembled according to the information conveyed in those copies.[9]

ADMISSIONS (SOME GRUDGING) OF

LIFE'S APPARENT DESIGN

THE VERY BEST MILLER-UREY CHEMISTRY, AS WE HAVE SEEN, DOES NOT TAKE US VERY FAR ALONG THE PATH TO A LIVING ORGANISM. A MIXTURE OF SIMPLE CHEMICALS, EVEN ONE ENRICHED WITH A FEW AMINO ACIDS, NO MORE RESEMBLES A BACTERIUM THAN A SMALL PILE OF REAL AND NONSENSE WORDS,

EACH WRITTEN ON AN INDIVIDUAL SCRAP
OF PAPER, RESEMBLES THE COMPLETE
WORKS OF SHAKESPEARE.

—ROBERT SHAPIRO[10]

JUST AS THERE IS NO ABSOLUTE BARRIER TO A
GROUNDHOG CROSSING A THOUSAND-LANE
HIGHWAY DURING RUSH HOUR, SO THERE IS NO
ABSOLUTE BARRIER TO THE PRODUCTION OF
PROTEINS, NUCLEIC ACIDS, OR ANY OTHER
BIOCHEMICAL BY IMAGINABLE, NATURAL CHEMICAL
PROCESSES; HOWEVER, THE SLAUGHTER ON
THE HIGHWAY IS UNBEARABLE.

—MICHAEL J. BEHE[11]

THE QUEST TO UNDERSTAND HOW THE SPARK OF
LIFE IGNITES FROM NON-LIFE IS ONE AREA OF
RESEARCH THAT HAS SO FAR TURNED UP MORE
SMOKE THAN FIRE.

—DAVID KOERNER AND SIMON LEVAY[12]

THE BELIEF THAT LIFE ON EARTH AROSE
SPONTANEOUSLY FROM NON-LIVING MATTER,
IS SIMPLY A MATTER OF FAITH IN STRICT
REDUCTIONISM AND IS BASED
ENTIRELY ON IDEOLOGY.

—HUBERT YOCKEY[13]

THE CURRENT SCENARIO OF THE ORIGIN OF LIFE IS ABOUT AS LIKELY AS THE ASSEMBLAGE OF A 747 BY A TORNADO WHIRLING THROUGH A JUNKYARD.
—FRED HOYLE, FAMED ASTRONOMER[14]

I THINK IT QUITE POSSIBLE THAT LIFE IS SO EXTREMELY IMPROBABLE THAT NOTHING CAN "EXPLAIN" WHY IT ORIGINATED.
—KARL POPPER, PHILOSOPHER OF SCIENCE[15]

AN HONEST MAN, ARMED WITH ALL THE KNOWLEDGE AVAILABLE TO US NOW, COULD ONLY STATE THAT IN SOME SENSE, THE ORIGIN OF LIFE APPEARS AT THE MOMENT TO BE ALMOST A MIRACLE, SO MANY ARE THE CONDITIONS WHICH WOULD HAVE HAD TO HAVE BEEN SATISFIED TO GET IT GOING.
—FRANCIS CRICK (CODISCOVERER OF THE DOUBLE HELIX STRUCTURE OF DNA)[16]

The incredibly organized, coordinated structures of life at the biochemical level are not just hard to explain naturalistically. They actually cry out to be explained as the product of someone's deliberate, intelligent action. The origin of life is evidence for God, not merely because it is difficult to explain without God, but because an intelligent Creator is the most reasonable explanation. We will explore this point in the next chapter.

For Further Reading

Thaxton, Charles B., Walter L. Bradley, and Roger L. Olsen. *The Mystery of Life's Origin: Reassessing Current Theories.* New York: Philosophical Library, 1984. Three scientists explain why naturalistic theories of life's origin are proving unworkable.

Shapiro, Robert. *Origins: A Skeptic's Guide to the Creation of Life on Earth.* New York: Summit Books, 1986. While refusing even to consider the possibility of a Creator (p. 119), Shapiro masterfully explains why naturalistic explanations of the origin of life are not holding up scientifically.

7

THE EVIDENCE OF LIFE'S INTELLIGENT DESIGN

> THE CLOSER WE LOOK, THE
> CLEARER IT IS THAT LIFE WAS
> INTELLIGENTLY DESIGNED.

OK, OK, you may be saying—it's amazing that our universe, solar system, and the Earth are just precisely what they need to be for life to exist. And it's extremely difficult to explain how life could get going, even here on our wonderful planet. But why bring God into the picture? Why not hold out the hope that science will find an explanation for all these mysterious, wonderful coincidences that does not involve a supernatural Creator? A fair question and one that we will answer in this chapter.

I will give thanks to You, for I am fearfully
and wonderfully made; Wonderful are
Your works, And my soul knows it very well.

—DAVID (PSALM 139:14 NASB)

ACCIDENTAL OR DELIBERATE:

YOU *CAN* TELL THE DIFFERENCE

To assert that God created life is to say that the One who brought the universe into existence also did something with the deliberate purpose of bringing life into existence. But can science say anything about an event being the result of a deliberate or purposeful act?

Yes, it can. When we think of science, we usually think of the study of natural events and processes—things that happen without being purposefully guided or directed. For example, we think of the study of lava flows in geology or of tumor growths in medicine. However, the more we learn about such unguided processes, the more we are able to distinguish them from guided processes or events. As William Dembski puts it, "Precisely because of what we know about undirected natural causes and their limitations, science is now in a position to demonstrate design rigorously."[1]

Dembski, a Baylor University professor, is a pioneer in the movement commonly called Intelligent Design (ID). Dembski points out that many modern sciences and other professional disciplines have highly developed methods for "distinguishing intelligent causes from undirected natural causes."[2] For example, when a man is found dead, the police detectives investigating the death will want to determine if the death was the result of (a) natural causes, (b) an accident, or (c) a deliberate act. The science of forensics is a multidisciplinary system of investigative methods and tools for making such a determination.

Or consider the science of archaeology. When archaeologists find an unusually shaped object at a site, they will seek to determine if natural processes formed the object or if, instead, humans shaped or constructed something for a specific purpose. Even the SETI (search for extraterrestrial intelligence) programs use scientifically based, objective criteria for distinguishing naturally occurring radio signals of space from possible transmissions by alien civilizations. Whenever an insurance company determines that someone deliberately wrecked an automobile or a copyright office determines that someone plagiarized a particular book, they employ similar reasoning.[3] In all of these kinds of investigations, the possibility of intelligent, purposeful causes—however mundane (such as murderers) or extraordinary (such as extraterrestrials) they may seem—is taken seriously.

> N.A.S.A.'S SEARCH FOR EXTRA-TERRESTRIAL INTELLIGENCE (S.E.T.I.) PRESUPPOSED THAT INFORMATION IMBEDDED IN ELECTROMAGNETIC SIGNALS FROM SPACE WOULD INDICATE AN INTELLIGENT SOURCE. AS YET, HOWEVER, RADIO-ASTRONOMERS HAVE NOT FOUND INFORMATION-BEARING SIGNALS COMING FROM SPACE. BUT CLOSER TO HOME, MOLECULAR BIOLOGISTS HAVE IDENTIFIED ENCODED INFORMATION IN THE CELL.
> —STEPHEN C. MEYER[4]

The central insight of Intelligent Design theory is that the same type of reasoning can be applied to the study of life. When seeking to explain the origin of life, or the origin of some structure or feature of living things (such as the eye), we should not assume that unguided natural processes alone will give a complete explanation. Rather, we should consider the possibility that they originate as the result of deliberate action by an intelligent agent. William Dembski has developed what he calls an "explanatory filter" that allows investigators in any discipline, including the sciences, to differentiate actual instances of design from other unusual occurrences.[5]

Dembski's filter consists of three stages of inquiry. First, we may ask whether a particular occurrence was naturally *necessary* or *contingent*. An occurrence is naturally necessary if the natural laws governing the physical objects involved are sufficient to explain the occurrence. To illustrate the difference, let's return to our Scrabble analogy from the previous chapter. If a hundred Scrabble tiles are lying on a smooth linoleum floor, the fact that all one hundred of them are lying flat is exactly what we would expect from the laws of physics. So, such an occurrence is naturally necessary. On the other hand, if all of the tiles are lying faceup, that is not a situation necessitated by the laws of physics. If you dump the tiles on the floor, it's quite possible (and even likely) for some of them to land facedown. So this occurrence is naturally contingent.

If an occurrence is determined to be contingent, we may move on to the second stage of the explanatory filter. At this stage we ask whether the occurrence is *simple* or *complex*. Finding the words *THE* or *BUT* or even *DOES* on the floor, formed by adjacent Scrabble tiles, would be examples of simple occurrences. On the other hand, finding words linked together in crossword fashion that happen to form Mark Twain's sentence "Everybody talks about the weather but nobody does anything about it" is a very different matter. This is a highly complex arrangement.

Complexity in and of itself does not, however, prove design. Dembski's third stage of inquiry seeks to distinguish genuine instances of design from other highly complex phenomena. In this third stage, we ask whether the pattern inherent in the complex occurrence is *ad hoc* or *specific.* An ad hoc pattern is one that really has no meaning or signifi-cance outside the single occurrence in which it is found. For example, suppose just twenty of our hundred Scrabble tiles form the following arrangement:

| N | D | E | O | K | N | A | M | U | E | A | R | N | B | A | O | S | R | R | E |

The above arrangement of letters is certainly complex. Furthermore, the probability of this particular arrangement occurring is rather remote—about one in twenty trillion quadrillion (26^{20} is roughly equal to 2×10^{28}). Nevertheless, there it is! It would be pointless to ask why this arrangement of twenty letters occurred rather than some other arrangement. The above arrangement has no significance other than it just happens to be the one chosen here. Furthermore, the fact that some meaningful, simple words can be picked out (OK, EAR, EARN) is insignificant, because these words do not form a complex, meaningful whole. (We arranged the letters randomly, with no intention of these particular words showing up.)

Note that an arrangement using twenty letters with a high degree of order would not necessarily prove design. For example, consider the following arrangement of twenty letters:

B	E	B	E	B	E	B	E	B	E	B	E	B	E	B	E	B	E	B	E

The above arrangement also is one in twenty trillion quadrillion possible outcomes, but is obviously not random. On the other hand, though, it is highly *simple.* Remember that in order to be sure of design, the occurrence must be complex. (Of course, a simple occurrence could be designed, but we are asking about *proving* design.) To prove design, then, we would need to find a complex occurrence that also has a highly meaningful order, such as the following:

O	U	R	N	A	M	E	S	A	R	E	K	E	N	A	N	D	R	O	B

The above arrangement of letters has the same bare "probability" as any other outcome among the roughly twenty trillion quadrillion possible arrangements of twenty letters in a row. However, what the above arrangement has is a *specificity* that the vast majority of such arrangements do not have. It has a specific meaning or significance apart from the letters themselves, apart from any event involving Scrabble tiles falling on a floor. In fact, the arrangement here uses the same twenty letters as in our first example but places them in this unique, meaningful order. The more meaningful statement of probability is that only about one in a billion quadrillion arrangements of twenty letters will have *any specific meaning at all.*[6]

DEMBSKI'S EXPLANATORY FILTER FOR DETECTING DESIGN[7]

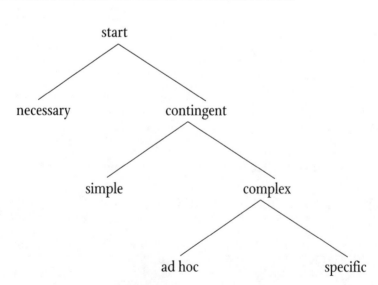

RUN THIS THROUGH YOUR SPELLCHECKER . . .

The application of intelligent design theory to life is fairly straightforward. On a multiplicity of levels, life exhibits a highly complex, specified order that cannot be explained as the inevitable outcome of natural processes. The point may be illustrated with DNA. A DNA macromolecule uses a complex structure that looks a bit like a very, very long spiral staircase or ladder (called the double helix). Each "step" or "rung" is formed by pairing up two of the four nucleotides (molecules containing nitrogen) found in DNA called adenine (A), thymine (T), cytosine (C), and guanine (G). When cells reproduce, the two rails or strands (which consist of sugar and phosphate molecules) untwist and separate from each other, then reconnect to other strands to form exact duplicates of the original.

For DNA work, it is not enough to have lots of As, Ts, Cs, and Gs (like a large collection of Scrabble letters) strung together. That would be like having Scrabble tiles lined up to spell nonsense words. The nucleotides must be strung together in a precise order and the two strands matched up to convey information to the rest of the cell that determines its overall structure, properties, and functions. In other words, the nucleotides must be arranged in a highly specific and highly complex order that conveys meaningful instructions. They function just like letters in a sentence—except that, given the length and complexity of a typical DNA double helix, a better comparison would be the letters that form a chapter or even a book.

Let us, then, apply Dembski's explanatory filter to DNA. The laws of physics and chemistry are woefully inadequate to explain the origin of DNA as a necessary product of any particular physical occurrences or series of chemical reactions. They certainly cannot explain the information content of DNA. Suppose for the sake of argument that DNA could form spontaneously through some series of unguided chemical reactions (which seems extraordinarily unlikely). Even if such a thing could occur, it would not explain the *meaning* of the information conveyed by the DNA coding. In the same way, if a coherent sentence were to form when a box of Scrabble tiles was dropped on the floor, the physics governing the motions of the tiles would not explain the meaning of the sentence. (For example, "OUR NAMES ARE KEN AND ROB" has a meaning that cannot be reduced to "A certain group of Scrabble tiles happened to fall in this way.") Thus, the informational content of DNA must be deemed naturally contingent rather than necessary.

Second, it is undeniable that the information conveyed by DNA is extremely complex; it is not at all like a simple "BEBEBEBE" but is very much like a set of blueprints for the construction of a factory's series of machines. Third, the complexity of DNA has a highly ordered, meaningfully specific complexity. Again, it is comparable to a lengthy manual or a cookbook or a set of blueprints, with numerous precise specifications that are intricately coordinated. We have, then, good reason to infer that DNA was intelligently designed and not the result of purely unguided, unplanned natural processes.

IF THE SHOE FITS, WHO MADE IT?

This character of complex specificity is not limited to the molecular components of life. Rather, it is found at every level of life from the single-cell organism to the human body. The more biologists learn about living organisms, the more they are discovering what Michael Behe calls *irreducible complexity:* "An irreducibly complex system is one that requires several closely matched parts in order to function and where removal of one of the components effectively causes the system to cease functioning."[8] Behe's favorite nonbiological illustration of irreducible complexity is a mousetrap, which consists minimally of a platform, a hammer, a spring, a catch, and a holding bar, each of which must be at the right size and position relative to the other parts for the whole to function at all.[9]

Let's consider two of Behe's best-known illustrations of irreducible complexity in life. (Keep in mind that our layman's descriptions make these features sound much *simpler* than they actually are.) Certain bacteria can move in water by using *flagella*—hairlike filaments imbedded in the outer wall of the bacterium. Electron microscopes have enabled researchers to discover amazing features of the flagella. Each flagellum acts as a rotary propeller, churning in the water in sync with the other flagella to move the bacterium in the desired direction. Each flagellum is attached to the cell wall by a "hook protein" that Behe likens functionally to a universal joint. At the base of each flagellum are several rings that evidently function as parts of a rotary motor. The flagellum thus works like a microscopic motorboat in which its three fundamental parts—a propeller, a motor, and a rotor—form an irreducibly complex system.[10]

THE ROTARY PROPELLER SYSTEM OF THE BACTERIUM E. COLI[11]

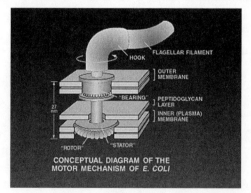

Behe's other celebrated example of irreducible complexity is the process called blood clotting. You may not have thought about it much, but whenever you get a cut, you bleed; and if the blood kept flowing out of your cut, you'd die. But that doesn't happen (except in bodies with diseases such as hemophilia). Instead, the blood congeals or thickens along the entire line of the cut and hardens just enough to stop the loss of blood. Meanwhile, the blood continues to pump normally throughout the circulatory system inside the body. It turns out that blood clotting is an extremely complex process involving a long list of proteins that do different jobs, each of which is essential to getting the blood to clot at the right time and place and in the right amount. If some of these proteins were missing (say, in a hypothetical earlier stage in the evolution of the blood clotting system), either blood clotting would not occur at all, or it would not turn off (thus congealing all of the blood in the organism). Behe likens imaginative scenarios of the gradual evolution of a functioning blood clotting system to a man shuffling a deck and dealing one perfect bridge hand after another: "Blood coagulation is a paradigm of the staggering complexity that underlies even apparently simple bodily processes."[12]

TO A PERSON WHO DOES NOT FEEL OBLIGATED TO
RESTRICT HIS SEARCH TO UNINTELLIGENT CAUSES,
THE STRAIGHTFORWARD CONCLUSION IS THAT
MANY BIOCHEMICAL SYSTEMS WERE DESIGNED.
—MICHAEL BEHE[13]

DESIGN: THE BEST EXPLANATION

The argument that we are presenting here is not merely that the
origin of life and its irreducibly complex systems are hard to explain as
the result of natural processes alone. Such an argument would remain
open to the response that perhaps scientists will one day find such an
explanation. The point that we are making is that the *best* explanation
for the information-rich nature of life is that it was intelligently
designed. Science has at its disposal tools of inquiry that make it possible to reach informed, strongly supported conclusions as to whether or
not a particular phenomenon or occurrence was the result of the purposeful action of an intelligent agent. We use those tools to distinguish
an interesting natural rock formation from a Mount Rushmore or to
distinguish accidental deaths from acts of murder or to distinguish a
random series of noises from a message sent in Morse code. The same

tools of inquiry make it possible for us to discern with reasonable confidence that life was designed.

FOR FURTHER READING

Behe, Michael J. *Darwin's Black Box: The Biochemical Challenge to Evolution.* New York: The Free Press, 1996. Groundbreaking work that makes a strong case for irreducible complexity in living things, especially on the cellular level.

Dembski, William A. *Mere Creation: Science, Faith and Intelligent Design.* Downers Grove, Ill.: InterVarsity Press, 1998. Perhaps the best introduction to intelligent design theory, including papers by Dembski, Behe, and several other leading thinkers in the movement.

8

THE EVIDENCE OF A FALLEN WORLD

AS WONDERFUL AS IT CAN BE, IT'S
OBVIOUS THAT NOT ALL IS RIGHT
WITH THE WORLD.

Critics of Christianity have a standard rebuttal to the argument for

God's existence from the intelligent design of the universe and of life:

not everything seems to work as it should. To put it bluntly, bad things

happen. Many people think that the bad things that happen negate any

apparent evidence of God's care and that these bad things raise serious

doubts about God existing at all.

Right off, we wish to make it clear that we don't pretend to know

why each and every particular bad thing happens. Nor will we try in this

chapter to offer a complete answer to the "problem of evil," as it is often

called. There's a lot written on this subject already for those who wish to pursue the matter.[1] Instead, we want to look at this question in another way—one that may surprise you. We want to argue that your very recognition that bad things happen is evidence for the Christian belief in God. To put it another way, we think that the state of affairs when it comes to good and evil is exactly what Christianity claims. In this chapter, we'll explain why.

[God] makes his sun rise on the evil and on the good, and sends rain on the just and on the unjust.

—JESUS (MATTHEW 5:45)

PEOPLE ARE GENIUSES—AND IDIOTS

We human beings are perhaps the greatest mystery of the cosmos. On the one hand, alone among all known species of life on Earth, we have a capacity for higher-ordered reasoning. By that we mean that human beings alone have the capacity for *thinking about thinking*. We don't claim that horses or chimpanzees, for example, can't think. In some ways, we are finding out that some animals have a significant capacity for various kinds of learning. But no other form of life that we know of engages in thoughtful reflection. No other species asks questions (aloud or, as best we can tell, silently to themselves) like, "How do I know that such-and-such is true?" or "Why do I believe this way rather than that way?" Certain animals may be able to learn how to count or even perform basic arithmetical computations; but no animal can wonder whether mathematics corresponds to anything in the real world. For all we know, animals may enjoy a beautiful sunset, but they don't think about the meaning of beauty. In this respect, at least, and probably in other related respects, human beings have a mental capacity that is qualitatively different from and superior to anything that other living things on Earth possess.

On the other hand, people often do really stupid things. In recent years Wendy Northcutt has been cataloguing egregious examples of human stupidity in her "Darwin Awards." A Pennsylvania man refused to go to the hospital after being bitten by a cobra, choosing to go to a bar, where he finished three drinks before dying from the poison. A Ukrainian fisherman ran electrical cables from his house into the river in order to electrocute the fish, then waded into the river to collect the fish without removing the cable, thus electrocuting himself. A Florida salesman crashed and died when he was reading his sales manual while driving eighty miles an hour on Interstate 95.[2] Northcutt's Darwin

Award winners, she wryly comments, "contrive to eliminate themselves from the gene pool in such an extraordinarily idiotic manner, that their action ensures the long-term survival of our species, which now contains one less idiot."[3]

No other species exhibits both astounding intelligence and astonishing idiocy as the human race. Nor should this observation be construed as dividing humanity into the brainy and the brainless. High-school dropouts can make shrewd decisions; college graduates can make dumb mistakes. If you've ever said to yourself, "How could I be so stupid," then you know that you're affected by the same mysterious, paradoxical inconsistency. We sure are!

People Are Good—and Evil

What we have been saying about intelligence applies equally to human beings with regard to moral conduct. On the one hand, human beings have an enormous capacity for good. This capacity seems to be related to our capacity for reflection about the meaning of things. People don't just think about sending donations to the Red Cross or about running into a burning building to rescue others in danger; they think about the *value* of such behavior. Animals may do good things, but they don't appear to have the capacity for thinking about what makes a particular behavior good. Human beings have the ability to weigh the interests of others against their own self-interest and to decide to give of themselves sacrificially, not out of instinct but out of conviction.

On the other hand, human beings have an obvious capacity for evil. War may be the most obvious manifestation of that capacity. As Charles Van Doren points out in *A History of Knowledge,* whereas combat between individual males is not uncommon in other species, "War is waged by few or none of the animals that share the earth with man. . . . No species of larger animals or birds undertakes campaigns of extermination against other members of the same species."[4]

For Americans, two dates in our own lifetime epitomize the evil that people can do. On April 19, 1995, at about 9:02 A.M. local time, a Ryder truck rigged with a bomb was exploded next to the Murrah Federal Building in Oklahoma City, killing 168 people—many of them children at a day-care center in the building. At the time, the event was the worst incident of terrorism in American history.[5]

Six years later, on September 11, 2001, at about 8:44 A.M. local time, the first of two airplanes was crashed deliberately into the north tower of the World Trade Center buildings in New York City. The second airliner plunged into the south tower at about 9:03 A.M. Later that morning, another plane was crashed into the Pentagon, while a fourth crashed in a field in western Pennsylvania after passengers fought with the hijackers to prevent another deliberate attack. In all, just over 3,000 people were killed, all but about 200 of them at the World Trade Center site.

These tragic events illustrate all too painfully the capacity for evil in the human race. They also illustrate the capacity for good, since in both cases, as in events of this kind generally, many people stepped forward to help at the risk of their own lives. In their attempt to save lives, some 343 firefighters and 23 police officers are reported to have died during the aftermath of the World Trade Center attacks.

Again, though, we must be careful not to use events like these to divide humanity too simplistically into the moral and the immoral or the good and the evil. Yes, some people are notoriously bad, and some people are notably good. But very bad people can do some good things, and very good people have been known to do some bad things. Caring, hard-working ministers sometimes commit adultery with parishioners or, as in recent scandals in the Roman Catholic Church in the U.S., molest children from their congregations. Politicians sometimes accept illegal campaign contributions or obstruct justice so that they can continue to work for political causes that they sincerely believe benefit the citizens they represent.

> IT IS BECOMING MORE AND MORE OBVIOUS THAT IT IS NOT STARVATION, NOT MICROBES, NOT CANCER, BUT MAN HIMSELF WHO IS MANKIND'S GREATEST DANGER.
>
> —CARL GUSTAV JUNG

A particularly distressing recent case is that of Andrea Yates, the Texas woman sentenced to life in prison for drowning her five children (the oldest of whom was seven) in the bathtub on June 20, 2001. Whatever one thinks of her defense—that she was mentally ill at the time—there can be no justification for denying that what she did was a horrible evil. Yet her husband could still say of her after the sentencing that she was "the kindest and most caring person I know."[6]

Yates's story is just one example of the universal fact that human beings have an enormous capacity for both good and evil. If we're honest with ourselves, we'll admit that we've not only said and done some pretty stupid things, we've also done some pretty bad things. Perhaps we never have killed anyone, but we've probably lost our temper at people and hurt them either physically with our hands or emotionally with our words. Most of us have never molested little children, but far too many of us have cheated in one way or another on our spouses. And it's a sure bet that we haven't always done the good that we could have done for others. When we are young, even if we're not bullies, we may stand by and say nothing while bullies pick on kids smaller than them. When we are old, even if we don't abuse children, we may fail to cherish them. Whatever our own personal failings, it's certain that we all have them.

> I HAVE MORE TROUBLE WITH D. L. MOODY
> THAN WITH ANY OTHER MAN I'VE EVER MET.
> —D. L. MOODY

Different religions and philosophies have developed several theories to explain human nature. We will consider the three most prevalent and important of these theories and ask which of them best fits the evidence.

ATHEISM: STUFF JUST HAPPENS

The atheists' usual explanation for the mystery of humanity's capacity for both good and evil is that the judgments "good" and "evil" are our own conventional ways of speaking about things that we humans find tolerable or intolerable. Mass murder and war are bad because they threaten the stability of our lives or of our species, and we're rather attached to our species! Likewise, we applaud acts of heroism and efforts to bring peace because they make our lives more secure. But these judgments, according to atheism, are not based on any absolute or transcendent values. In their view, the reality is that good and evil are human conventions, or even fictions, that we use to encourage behavior that we want and discourage behavior that we don't want.

This typical atheistic view of good and evil is inadequate for at least two reasons. First, it doesn't really explain the glories of human goodness or the shamefulness of human evil. As we have noted, human beings seem to have a capacity for both good and evil that is qualitatively greater than and different from anything we see in other living things on Earth. Like the character in Henry Wadsworth Longfellow's poem about a little girl, when we're good, we're very, very good, but when we're bad, we're horrid. Atheism really cannot explain this. How did such a wildly unpredictable, unstable species evolve?

Second, atheism's explanation for why we should prefer certain behaviors over others falls short of meeting what most people, at any rate, know about right and wrong. Most of us know that molesting little children is not merely an undesirable activity because it introduces some instability into the community of our species. We know that in itself it is a despicable, horrible act. Why that should be so, if we are merely another animal species, is difficult to understand—just as it is difficult to understand why so many males of our species do it. Likewise, most of us understand that rescuing children or old people from a burning building is not just a boon to the species. We know that such acts are good, period.

Please understand that we are not suggesting that atheists can't do good things. They can, and they often do. What we are suggesting is that atheism as a philosophy doesn't do a good job of explaining why people should do good things and shouldn't do bad things.

PANTHEISM: *QUE SERA, SERA*

Pantheists typically regard good as absolute reality but evil as an illusion. This doesn't mean, generally, that pantheists deny that nations wage wars or that spouses cheat on each other. Rather, pantheists usually explain that we view such occurrences as evil because we assume that the material world is real and that what happens to our bodies is important. For pantheists, especially in the context of Eastern religions, these assumptions are questionable. Any reality that pantheists accord to the material world is derivative and dependent upon the unseen spiritual reality in which we are all one, in which we are all divine, and in which we are all good. The separateness or individuality of our bodily existence is itself an illusion, in this view—one that drives us to act selfishly.[7]

Pantheism comes in a variety of forms, but all of them have one very serious problem in the matter of explaining good and evil. Pantheism cannot explain why, if we are all perfectly good and divine and one with each other, we are acting selfishly and suffering from this illusion of separateness. How can the divine manifest the demonic?

Even panentheism, the more philosophically sophisticated worldview that views God as the soul or mind of the cosmos, has trouble at this point. If the divine Mind in all things is good, how can the things in which that good Mind dwells do such bad things?

Pantheism also has had difficulty historically making a strong case for why people should choose to do good and not do bad. If pantheism is true, then everything that happens is in some sense a manifestation of the divine. Furthermore, if pantheism is true, we're all going to "make it" because we're all part of the divine. Therefore, if someone's path to the realization of their own divinity involves them in wrongdoing, ultimately that's OK.

Again, we don't mean to suggest that pantheists approve of wrongdoing or that they can't be kind and decent people. Far from it. But pantheism has great difficulty explaining why so many people do such horribly bad things.

THEISM: SPOILED BRATS, SPOILED WORLD

If no God exists at all, it is hard to see what basis we would find on which the world could be considered good or bad. If God is all or in all, it is hard to see why anything bad would ever happen. The evidence for the intelligent, beautiful design of the universe and of life on Earth strongly militates against atheism; the evidence of humanity's often unintelligent, ugly behavior strongly militates against pantheism.

Flaws and defects in a highly ordered, apparently well-designed world are best explained as the result of a good world being somehow *spoiled*. This is exactly what theism says is the case. God made the world perfectly good (as Genesis 1 says repeatedly) and created us with the capacity for choices based on reflective thought. That capacity for thoughtful, deliberate choice is a good thing, but it's capable of being abused. According to theism, human beings abused that capacity and have chosen as a species to try to handle life without God. We are alienated from one another, from the animals, and from God. The results have been disastrous. Like spoiled children, we have thrown collective tantrums, demanded our own way, and gotten out of line. In the process, we have been making a colossal mess of the home God made for us.

Most cultures and religions bear testimony to the awareness that things haven't always been like this. Our present condition is not our original condition. Confucianism recalls a golden age of civility when children respected their elders and everyone was happy in their relationships with one another. Taoism recalls a distant past when human beings were in sync with nature. What these and other religions do not recognize is that our loss of that ancient innocence and purity arises from our estrangement from God.

We conclude, then, that the biblical view that God created a good world that has been corrupted by our bad choices is the best explanation of all the evidence. It explains the presence of both good and evil and our awareness of it in other humans as well as in ourselves. This evidence for the existence of God is especially compelling, since we experience it in our own lives every day.

For Further Reading

Lewis, C. S. *Mere Christianity*. New York: Macmillan, 1952; reprint, San Francisco: Harper, 2001. See chapter 1, "Right and Wrong as a Clue to the Meaning of the Universe," for a wonderful treatment of the question.

Moreland, J. P., and David M. Ciocchi, eds. *Christian Perspectives on Being Human: A Multidisciplinary Approach to Integration*. Grand Rapids: Baker, 1993. A stimulating collection of essays defending and exploring the Christian view of human nature.

9

THE EVIDENCE OF THE
BIBLE'S RELIABILITY

THE GENERAL RELIABILITY OF THE
BIBLE'S TEXT AND MAJOR "STORY
LINE" IS NOT IN QUESTION.

So far we have considered evidence for God's existence that is in principle accessible to everyone. While this evidence gives us good reasons to believe that a God exists, it doesn't tell us exactly who God is or what He wants. Christianity is based on the understanding that God has not left the world in the dark about these things. He has revealed himself in the Bible. He has told us who He is, why we're here, what's gone wrong with us and our world, and how He has gone about making things right.

The grass withers, the flower fades; but
the word of our God will stand forever.

—ISAIAH 40:8

How reliable, though, is the information in the Bible?

WHAT YOU READ IS WHAT THEY WROTE

Let's start with a common misconception. Many people have the idea that in the process of copying and recopying the books of the Bible, century after century, some parts got lost, other parts got added, and now no one really knows what the Bible originally said about anything. This is a myth. The original text of every book of the Bible has been remarkably preserved, and its message is still able to come through quite clearly.

Three facts about the manuscript copies give us cause for confidence that the original text of the books of the Bible has been successfully passed down to us. First, we have plenty of ancient manuscripts of the Bible, both for the Hebrew Old Testament and for the Greek New

Testament. For example, we have thousands of Hebrew Old Testament manuscripts that have been found all over Europe and the Middle East, including an especially fabulous collection discovered by scholars in Cairo in 1896. We also have the Dead Sea Scrolls, the first of which were discovered in 1947 and which include some two hundred Old Testament manuscripts. Likewise, we have hundreds of copies of each book of the New Testament in a mass of over five thousand Greek manuscripts found in museums and libraries worldwide.

> THE SCROLLS HAVE SHOWN THAT OUR TRADITIONAL BIBLE HAS BEEN AMAZINGLY ACCURATELY PRESERVED FOR OVER 2,000 YEARS.
> —EUGENE ULRICH, EDITOR OF OXFORD UNIVERSITY'S DEAD SEA SCROLLS SERIES
> *DISCOVERIES IN THE JUDEAN DESERT*[1]

> THE VARIANT READINGS ABOUT WHICH ANY DOUBT REMAINS AMONG TEXTUAL CRITICS OF THE NEW TESTAMENT AFFECT NO MATERIAL QUESTION OF HISTORIC FACT OR OF CHRISTIAN FAITH AND PRACTICE.
> —F. F. BRUCE, UNIVERSITY OF MANCHESTER PROFESSOR OF NEW TESTAMENT[2]

Second, the quality of the manuscripts is very good. The discovery of the Dead Sea Scrolls gave concrete proof that the Jewish scribes had preserved the text with astonishing accuracy. The number of variant readings between the biblical Scrolls and the medieval manuscript tradition turned out to be quite small, and most of these are variations in spelling and style. The quality of the New Testament manuscripts, while not as good as that of the Old, is still very good—considerably better than the manuscript quality of other ancient documents. Where there are variant readings, in most cases scholars have no trouble deciding which variant represents the original.

Third, the time span between the originals and our earliest copies is unusually short for ancient writings. The discovery of the Dead Sea Scrolls, dating from about 200 B.C. to A.D. 68, drastically reduced the time span from the writing of the Old Testament books (between about 1400 and 400 B.C.) to our earliest copies of them. In addition, two small silver scrolls discovered at Ketef Hinnom (a site near Jerusalem) and dating from the seventh century B.C. contain the traditional priestly benediction worded almost exactly the same as in Numbers 6:24-26. This is a significant find not only for that small portion of text but also for showing that at least some of the priestly material of the Pentateuch dates from long before the Exile (when some skeptical scholars claim most of the Old Testament was written). The time span between the writing of the original New Testament books (between about A.D. 50 and

100) and our earliest manuscript copies is exceptionally short, as it includes manuscript fragments from the late first and early second centuries and whole books of the New Testament from the end of the second century.

To summarize, the Old and New Testaments enjoy far greater manuscript attestation in terms of quantity, quality, and time span than any other ancient documents. There is no reason to question the substantial accuracy and integrity of the texts of the Old and New Testament books as they have come down to us.

AND THAT'S THE WAY IT WAS...

Unlike most of the sacred writings of other religions, the Bible is largely a book of historical accounts of what God has done in the past (as well as explanations of what it all means). The truth of the Bible is therefore primarily a matter of the truth of its claims about certain crucial events that its writers assert happened in the history of Israel.

THE PATRIARCH NARRATIVES FIT COMFORTABLY
IN THE HISTORICAL CONTEXT THAT MODERN
ARCHAEOLOGY HAS HELPED TO RECONSTRUCT.
AND THAT CONTEXT PLACES THE PATRIARCHS
PRECISELY WHERE THE BOOK OF GENESIS
SUGGESTS THEY SHOULD BE—IN THE EARLY
SECOND MILLENNIUM BC—RATHER THAN IN
THE HANDS OF A POSTEXILIC FICTION WRITER.

—JEFFERY L. SHELER *(U.S. NEWS & WORLD REPORT* WRITER)[1]

The general outline of events narrated in the Bible, broadly speaking, has never been in serious doubt. The Israelites were a nation that from its earliest memories had a strong familial identity as the children of Abraham, Isaac, and Jacob. In every generation parents told their children, as they do to this day, of their bondage in Egypt and their escape to the Promised Land. Although Israel achieved some measure of military and economic strength about a thousand years before Jesus, it was short-lived: the kingdom of David and Solomon divided and the resulting two kingdoms were conquered, first the northern kingdom of Israel by the Assyrians in the eighth century B.C., then the southern kingdom of Judah in a wave of conquests by the Babylonians between 605 and 586 B.C. The Jewish Temple in Jerusalem, destroyed by the Babylonians, was rebuilt after the Jews were allowed to return by the

Persians, whose empire had supplanted the Babylonians in 539 B.C. Most if not all of the Old Testament was written by about four hundred years before Jesus, who was born about 4 B.C. Much of the Old Testament, especially in its latest books, spoke of a coming Deliverer and King from the family line of David who would bring the Israelites, as well as people of all nations, back to God.

> ALL THE INDICATIONS ARE THAT COURT SCRIBES
> CONSCIENTIOUSLY CHRONICLED THE MAIN EVENTS
> OF THESE TIMES [OF THE OLD TESTAMENT KINGS].
> THEIR ANNALS, NOW LOST, WERE TAKEN OVER BY
> THE COMPILERS OF THE SURVIVING BIBLICAL BOOKS,
> WHOSE PENCHANT FOR NATIONAL SELF-CRITICISM,
> MOST UNUSUAL AMONG THE ANCIENT WORLD'S
> SURVIVING RECORDS, FURTHER CORROBORATES
> THEIR STRONG CONCERN FOR TRUTH.
>
> —IAN WILSON, *THE BIBLE IS HISTORY*

During the four centuries between the Old and New Testaments, the Jews were ruled first by the Persians, then by the Greeks, and then, after about a century of independence, by the Romans. Jesus was an itinerant rabbi and reputed healer whose teaching offended some of the Jewish religious leadership of the day. He was eventually executed by order of Pontius Pilate, the Roman governor, just outside Jerusalem on or about the Jewish festival of Passover in either A.D. 30 or 33. A few weeks after His execution, Jesus' followers began proclaiming that He had risen from the dead, had appeared to them, and that he was the promised Deliverer-King, known in Hebrew as the *Messiah* and in Greek as the *Christ* ("anointed one"). About fifteen years later, Gentiles (or non-Jews) began to join the Church, as it was called. By A.D. 70, when the second Jewish Temple was destroyed in a war between the Jews and the Romans, the movement of Jesus' followers had become in effect a new religion, and its members became known as Christians.

Very little if any of the statements we have just made in summarizing the narrative of the Bible are disputed by historians or biblical scholars (of whatever religious background). Of course, skeptics question or deny most or all of the accounts of supernatural acts of God, or miracles. For that reason, some historians dismiss as mythological the Old Testament figures most directly associated with its most spectacular miracles, such as Moses. However, the general outline of the Bible's history is not in question. And almost no historian or scholar has ever argued that Jesus did not exist or that His original followers did not report having seen Him alive after His execution.

DIGGING UP DIRT ON THE BIBLE

The general historical reliability of the Bible may be corroborated through the discipline of archaeology. Here we must be cautious in not overstating the case. First of all, in the nature of things, archaeology cannot prove that Heaven exists or that the angel Gabriel visited Mary or that the Holy Spirit filled the apostles on Pentecost. Then again, no one has ever claimed that archaeology could "prove the Bible" in this sense.

More seriously, archaeology provides us with little direct physical evidence for most of the principal miraculous events reported in the Bible. The inscriptions, pottery, and other artifacts that archaeologists find from the ancient past always will be a very small fraction of what existed, providing, at best, scattered data that still needs to be interpreted and correlated with the historical writings from the period. We're not likely to find a diary of the Pharaoh of the Exodus recounting in detail the ten plagues and the destruction of his army in the Red Sea. On the other hand, we might find some Egyptian records referring to some of these events. In short, archaeology might be able to help us corroborate some of the biblical miracles, but we should not expect too much in this regard.

As you might expect, the information that can be derived from archaeology generally becomes fuller and easier to interpret the further forward in time that you look. The table on the next page illustrates this fact and gives a simple overview of what archaeology has been able to confirm for the different periods of biblical history. It shows that archaeology can confirm the general historical context of the older parts of the Bible and that specific historical details can be confirmed in greater number as we look closer to our own time.

BIBLICAL PERIOD	SUPPORT OUTSIDE THE BIBLE
Before Abraham (before about 2100 B.C.)	Archaeology can offer very little either for or against the biblical account. Writing was rare before Abraham.
Abraham, Isaac, Jacob, and Joseph (ca. 2100-1600 B.C.)	Archaeology and extrabiblical writings confirm many of the cultural details of the biblical account. Possible though debated references to biblical persons outside the Bible.
Moses, Joshua, and the Judges—the Exodus and the Conquest (ca. 1600-1100 B.C.)	Archaeology and extrabiblical writings show that events very much like those described in the Bible occurred (e.g., the Exodus plagues, the fall of Jericho's walls), but scholars have difficulty correlating the dates.
David and Solomon (ca. 1100-900 B.C.)	A couple of references to the House of David have been found, and distinctive features of the city of Jerusalem during the period have been confirmed in archaeological digs.
The Divided Kingdoms (ca. 900-600 B.C.)	The kings and nations that fought against Israel and Judah are known from extrabiblical sources. Dates for this period are generally

	considered settled to within several years or less. Skeptics rarely question the basic historical accuracy of the accounts for this period.
The Exile and Postexilic Period (ca. 600-400 B.C.)	Even more detailed correlations between biblical and pagan histories are possible for this period. Skeptics generally question only the overtly miraculous stories. Events can be dated to within a few years.
Between the Testaments (ca. 400-4 B.C.)	The historical books of the Apocrypha (written during this period) generally fit well with extrabiblical historical and archaeological data. Events can be dated to within one or two years.
Jesus and the Apostles— the New Testament (ca. 4 B.C.-A.D. 100)	Events reported in the Gospels and Acts fit extremely well with the historical and archaeological data. Various extrabiblical writings mention Jesus, John the Baptist, and specific facts about them. Events can be dated to within one or two years, sometimes better.

When you read the Bible, then, you are not reading something akin to Grimms' fairy tales or the ancient myths of the gods of Mount Olympus. While a certain amount of caution, even skepticism, about the reports of miracle and the details of the biblical narrative is understandable, there is no basis for wholesale skepticism of its historical claims. Any investigation or research into the historical accuracy of the Bible, then, is concerned with the crucial turning points in its history that are so hotly debated, not the overall general picture. In the next chapter, we will consider some of those contested historical claims of the biblical record.

FOR FURTHER READING

Geisler, Norman L., and William E. Nix. *A General Introduction to the Bible*, rev. ed. Chicago: Moody, 1986. A highly recommended textbook and reference work covering common questions concerning the origins of the Bible.

Wegner, Paul D. *The Journey from Texts to Translations: The Origin and Development of the Bible*. Grand Rapids: Baker Books, 1999. An excellent, up-to-date, and readable textbook on the origin and reliability of the text and collection of books of the Bible.

10

THE EVIDENCE OF THE BIBLE'S ACCURACY

WHERE WE CAN TEST THE BIBLE'S
ACCURACY IN MATTERS OF FACT, IT
HOLDS UP REMARKABLY WELL.

As we explained in the previous chapter, the general historical context and overall reliability of the Bible is not in serious question. The text of the Bible has been preserved with an extremely high degree of accuracy compared to other ancient literature so that we are confident that what we read reliably retains the wording and meaning of the original books of the Bible. There was an ancient nation of Israel, its people did manage to survive despite being conquered by a succession of major powers, and a man named Jesus did live in the first century and start a movement that came to regard Him as the crucified and resurrected Messiah of Israel.

This general reliability, however, is not a sufficient basis for accepting the remarkable claims of the Bible to be a revelation from God. We need to know if some of the more astounding claims of the Bible have any credibility to them. Is there evidence to support the Bible's historical accuracy in its most important claims?

We were not making up clever stories when we told you about the power of our Lord Jesus Christ and his coming again. We have seen his majestic splendor with our own eyes.

—PETER (2 PETER 1:16 NLT)

DID JOSHUA FIT THE BATTLE OF JERICHO?

The major historical claim of the Old Testament is that Israel originated from a series of miraculous events that enabled them to escape slavery in Egypt and to conquer the land of Canaan. Unfortunately, this claim is widely questioned today.

Old Testament archaeology is in a period of intense flux these days, largely due to problems with ancient chronology. A small but increasing number of historians and other researchers are questioning the standard chronologies for the various nations surrounding Israel in the ancient world, especially that of Egypt. The result is that mainstream archaeologists often proclaim that a particular biblical event did not happen as reported in the Old Testament because they can't find any evidence for it during the archaeological period in which they think it would have occurred. This is the real story behind the media-hyped stories of recent years proclaiming that archaeology has disproved the Bible.

Here's an interesting example. In 1995 *Time* magazine asked the question, "Did Joshua conquer the city of Jericho?" Their answer: "The walls of this Canaanite city did come tumbling down, say most historians, but centuries before Moses' protégé could have arrived."[1] In other words, that the walls of Jericho fell and the city was conquered in a manner consistent with the biblical account is now fairly clear from the archaeological evidence. What isn't clear is when exactly this happened and how the event can be correlated with the other historical information gleaned through archaeological discoveries across the Mediterranean and Middle East.

The same is true for the Exodus—the cluster of miraculous events through which the Israelites escaped from Egypt under the leadership of Moses. Egyptian writings record events that sound very familiar to readers of the Book of Exodus, even if many archaeologists ignore those reports because they don't fit the standard chronology. For example, the Admonitions of Ipuwer, an Egyptian writing dating from at least a thousand years before Jesus, appears to describe a number of the plagues, and the results are quite consistent with the Exodus:

Indeed, [hearts] are violent, pestilence is throughout the land, blood is everywhere, death is not lacking, and the mummy-cloth speaks even before one comes near it.

Indeed, many dead are buried in the river; the stream is a sepulcher and the place of embalmment has become a stream.

Indeed, noblemen are in distress, while the poor man is full of joy. Every town says: "Let us suppress the powerful among us.". . .

Indeed, the river is blood, yet men drink of it. Men shrink from human beings and thirst after water.

Indeed, gates, columns and walls are burnt up, while the hall of the palace stands firm and endures.

Indeed, the ship of [the southerners] has broken up; towns are destroyed and Upper Egypt has become an empty waste. . . .

Behold, men tread [the water] like fishes, and the frightened man cannot distinguish it because of terror. . . .

Indeed, gold and lapis lazuli, silver and turquoise, carnelian and amethyst, Ibhet-stone and [. . .] are strung on the necks of maidservants. . . .

Indeed, laughter is perished and is [no longer] made; it is groaning that is throughout the land, mingled with complaints. . . .

Indeed, all animals, their hearts weep; cattle moan because of the state of the land.

Indeed, the children of princes are dashed against walls, and the children of the neck are laid out on the high ground. . . .

Indeed, [men eat] herbage and wash [it] down with water; neither fruit nor herbage can be found [for] the birds, and [. . .] is taken away from the mouth of the pig. No face is bright which you have [. . .] for me through hunger.

Indeed, everywhere barley has perished and men are stripped of clothes, spice, and oil; everyone says: "There is none." The storehouse is empty and its keeper is stretched on the ground; a happy state of affairs!

Several of the ten plagues of the Exodus story are apparent here. The turning of the Nile river to blood (Exodus. 7:17-25) and the plague on the cattle (Exodus 9:1-7) are directly mentioned. The plague of hail and fire (Exodus 9:13-35) would explain the destruction of buildings and trees by fire mentioned in the Ipuwer text. The lack of fruit, herbs, and grain may be explained by the plague of locusts (Exodus 10:1-20). The reference to groaning throughout the land and the death of the children of princes fits the climactic tenth plague, the death of the firstborn sons of the Egyptians (Exodus 11:1-12:32). In addition, the text's reference to female slaves wearing jewelry recalls the plundering of the Egyptians by the Israelite slaves before leaving the land (Exodus 12:34-36). If the Ipuwer text was not describing the Exodus, it was describing something awfully similar to it.

The biblical accounts of the Exodus and Conquest, then, have surprising credibility. Though problems remain—as we would expect in studying such tumultuous events well over three thousand years ago—there are good reasons for viewing these events as historical, not mythical, in origin.

THE NEW TESTAMENT: EYEWITNESS NEWS

As for the New Testament, its credibility from an archaeological and historical point of view is above reproach. In later chapters we will consider the evidence for the most significant historical claims of the New Testament. Here we will focus on the historical credibility of two authors whose works comprise roughly half of the New Testament: Luke and Paul.

Historians have no trouble at all dovetailing the narrative of Luke's two works, the Gospel of Luke and the Book of Acts, with extrabiblical information, which is rather plentiful compared to the Old Testament period. For example, the Jewish historian Josephus confirms several events reported in Acts, including a famine in Judea during the reign of the Roman emperor Claudius (Acts 11:28) and the death of Herod Agrippa I (Acts 12:20-23). Josephus also mentions briefly John the Baptist, Jesus, and James the brother of Jesus. Not only does Josephus confirm their historical existence, but he confirms that Jesus was widely viewed as a wise man and a miracle worker and that He was put to death by order of Pontius Pilate based on accusations brought by some Jewish leaders.[3]

The detailed accuracy of Luke's two writings—the Gospel of Luke and the Book of Acts—has long been recognized.[4] He uses the proper titles for various officials throughout the Roman Empire: Herod the Great was called "tetrarch" (Luke 3:1), while his descendants Herod

Agrippa I and II were called "king" (Acts 12:1; 25:13). Luke knew that governors of senatorial provinces were called "proconsuls" (Cyprus, Acts 13:7; Achaia, Acts 18:12; Asia, Acts 19:38) and governors of imperial provinces were called "governors" (Luke 3:1; Acts 23:24; 26:30), and he knew which provinces were which. Luke shows a mastery of legal procedures in Jewish and Roman law at the time (especially in Acts 21-26), prompting A. N. Sherwin-White, a historian of Roman law, to comment concerning the Book of Acts, "Any attempt to reject its historicity even in matters of detail must now appear absurd. Roman historians have long taken it for granted."[5]

One of the key issues pertaining to the reliability of the Gospels and Acts is whether they were written close enough to the events to have preserved eyewitness testimony. Once again, the Book of Acts is pivotal. Some critics of the New Testament used to argue that Acts was written in the second century A.D., a claim that is easily disproved by the accuracy of its information, as we have just seen. But when *was* Acts written? The earliest possible date is about A.D. 60, since the book's narrative ends at that time. But that also appears to be very close to the actual date.

When the book ends, the apostle Paul is under house arrest in Rome, awaiting his appeal to Caesar. Sources outside the New

Testament show that Paul won his appeal and went free for another four or five years, when he returned to Rome and was martyred in the persecution of that same Caesar (Nero). It is very difficult to understand why Luke would stop his narrative at the point he did unless the outcome of Paul's appeal was still yet to be determined. Furthermore, the Book of Acts is largely focused on the defense of Paul's ministry. His conversion, when the risen Jesus appeared to him, is described at length in three essentially parallel accounts (Acts 9:1-19; 22:1-21; 26:1-23). Paul's travels and speeches dominate most of the book (Acts 13-28) and are reported with an emphasis on Paul's faithfulness to the Jewish Scriptures and his innocence under Roman law. It looks almost certain, then, that Acts was written while Paul was still alive and awaiting his appeal, perhaps in A.D. 61 or 62.

If Acts was written in the early 60s, though, then so was Luke's Gospel—and at least slightly earlier than Acts, since the Gospel was written first (see Acts 1:1). This means that Luke wrote his Gospel no more than about thirty years after Jesus' death. That's not much time for myths and legends to develop, and it's close enough that Luke could have had access to eyewitnesses—people who actually knew Jesus in the flesh and saw the things that Luke reports.

In any case, Luke clearly claims to have based his writings on eye-witness testimony (Luke 1:1-4). He tells us that he "investigated everything carefully" (Luke 1:3 NASB) and indicates that he has consulted other written sources on the subject matter. In Acts he even presents himself as a participant at times, referring to himself along with Paul and his other traveling companions as "we" in three extended passages (Acts 16:11-40; 20:5-21:26; 27:1-28:16). Given the impressive accuracy of his information and his apparent closeness to the events he reports, we ought to take his claim to be reporting eye-witness testimonies seriously.

The other writer about whom something may be said here is Paul himself. While some biblical scholars continue to question the early date of the 60s for Luke's writings, with Paul we can approach something like an undisputed bedrock of facts. Seven of the thirteen letters that bear Paul's name are agreed by all scholars to have been written by Paul (Romans, 1 and 2 Corinthians, Galatians, Philippians, 1 Thessalonians, and Philemon). Furthermore, there is no doubt about when Paul wrote these letters: between about A.D. 49 and 61. We therefore have a core of documents that all historians and scholars agree were written roughly twenty to thirty years after Jesus' death.

From Paul's undisputed epistles alone, various facts about early Christianity are easily documented beyond reasonable doubt. These include, first of all, that Jesus was a real person who was put to death on a Roman cross and that many of His original followers professed to have seen Him alive after His death and burial (1 Corinthians 15:3-7). Paul confirms the account of the Book of Acts that he also saw Jesus (1 Corinthians 15:8). He reports personal interactions with several Christian leaders mentioned in Acts, including Peter (whom Paul always calls by his Aramaic name Cephas), James the brother of Jesus, an eloquent preacher named Apollos, and Paul's protégés Timothy and Titus (1 Corinthians 1:12; 15:5-7; 16:10-12; 2 Corinthians 8:6, 16, 23; Galatians 1:18-19). Paul also provides details about his movements, including chronological data, which fit with the account in Acts (Romans 15:22-29; 2 Corinthians 2:12-13; Galatians 1:18-21; 2:1; etc.).

> I BELIEVE IN ONE GOD SOLE AND ETERNAL, WHO UNMOVED MOVES ALL THE HEAVENS WITH LOVE AND WITH DESIRE; AND FOR SUCH BELIEF I HAVE NOT ONLY PROOFS PHYSICAL AND METAPHYSICAL, BUT THAT TRUTH GIVES IT TO ME WHICH HENCE RAINS DOWN THROUGH MOSES, THROUGH PROPHETS AND WHATEVER PSALMS, THROUGH THE GOSPELS.
> —DANTE (*PARADISO*, CANTO XXIV, 125-132)

We have, then, significant evidence for concluding that the Bible gives us reliable, accurate historical information. While some skepticism about its miracle claims and its theological teachings may be understandable, there are strong reasons to reject a skeptical attitude toward the mundane historical accounts of the Bible. Within that context of historical credibility, the amazing claims of the biblical writers deserve a respectful hearing at least.

FOR FURTHER READING

Geisler, Norman L., and Ronald M. Brooks. *When Skeptics Ask.* Wheaton: Victor Books, 1990. Excellent popular-level discussion of questions about the reliability and accuracy of the Bible, with a helpful discussion of the problem of the dating of the Exodus and Conquest.

Sheler, Jeffery L. *Is the Bible True? How Modern Debates and Discoveries Affirm the Essence of the Scriptures.* San Francisco: Harper; Grand Rapids: Eerdmans, 1999. While denying that the Bible is perfectly accurate in all respects, Sheler, a reporter for U.S. News & World Report, shows that the Bible is credible and historically reliable.

11

THE EVIDENCE OF THE BIBLE'S FULFILLED PROPHECY

THE BIBLE CONTAINS REMARKABLE
PREDICTIONS OF EVENTS OCCUR-
RING CENTURIES LATER.

If the Bible were merely an ancient collection of writings that were historically credible, it would be interesting but probably not of ultimate significance. But the Bible claims to be much more—it claims to be the Word of God. From the Ten Commandments that Moses brought down from the Lord on Mount Sinai; to the oracles and messages of the prophets prefaced with the words, "Thus says the Lord"; to the authoritative words of Jesus, "Amen I say to you"; to the somber visions of the Book of Revelation, the Bible over and over again presents itself as the written expression of God revealing himself and speaking to humanity.

Of course, any book might *claim* to be divinely inspired; such a claim in and of itself proves nothing. But there is significant evidence to back up this claim. In this chapter we will highlight one such line of evidence, that of fulfilled prophecy in the Bible.

> *Declare and set forth your case;*
> *Indeed, let them consult together.*
> *Who has announced this from of old?*
> *Who has long since declared it?*
> *Is it not I, the LORD?*
>
> —ISAIAH 45:21 NASB

TAKING SKEPTICISM SERIOUSLY

Wait a minute, the skeptic says. Fulfilled prophecy proves the Bible? Right away, the skeptic will call foul on at least two grounds. First, skeptics allege that many biblical passages that appear to prophesy future events were actually written after the events in question. Imagine someone writing a book in the year 2002 that, for whatever reason, speaks of the 1963 assassination of John F. Kennedy as if it were a future event. Someone reading that book, say a thousand years from now, might mistakenly think that the book was really written before Kennedy's death and erroneously conclude that it was a real prediction.

Second, skeptics commonly allege that some or many of the events reported in the Bible as fulfillments of earlier prophecies were not actual historical events but pious fictions that the later authors invented. This allegation is the precise opposite of the first objection. According to the first objection, the reported event really did occur, but the "prophecy" was written after it, not before it. According to the second objection, the "prophecy" was written first, but the reported "event" did not actually take place. Obviously, skeptics can use both objections, but only one objection can apply to any particular apparent fulfilled prophecy. They can't have it both ways!

One might think that if skeptics are allowed to use either of these objections to any apparent fulfilled prophecy in the Bible as they choose, nothing would be left to serve as an example of fulfilled prophecy. However, this isn't the case. Give the skeptic every reasonable way out, and there is still considerable evidence of fulfilled prophecy in the Bible. We will look at historical events about which there is universal agree-ment among historians and compare them with biblical texts that schol-ars universally agree were written long before those events. What we will find is startling evidence that God really did speak through the prophets of the Bible.

Good News for the Whole World

Biblical prophecy, contrary to the way some zealous advocates regrettably portray it, is not about deciphering vague sayings or looking for coded references to various unrelated events in history. We're not talking Nostradamus here. Biblical prophecy at its heart is an unfolding story of God's working to bring people throughout the world into an authentic, life-transforming relationship with Him.

We could start with any number of places, but for our purposes we will start with Abraham. You only have to read a dozen chapters of the Bible to find an astonishing claim that sets the tone for the whole Bible and that began to be fulfilled in earnest only during the New Testament era. According to Genesis, the Lord told Abraham:

I will make you a great nation;
I will bless you
And make your name great;

And you shall be a blessing.
I will bless those who bless you,
And I will curse him who curses you;
And in you all the families of the earth shall be blessed.

—GENESIS 12:2-3 NKJV

Now, let's give the skeptics every conceivable advantage here. Although Genesis is traditionally attributed to Moses in the fifteenth century B.C., let's date Genesis 12 to the latest possible time according to the most radical scholarly opinion, which would be in the fifth century B.C. (Even most skeptical scholars generally think this part of Genesis dates from considerably earlier, but we can afford to be generous.) By that time, Israel—the nation that had come from Abraham and that produced the Old Testament—had already seen its most glorious days under David and Solomon. (In fact, some biblical scholars date this part of Genesis to a time not long after Solomon.) So the skeptic could explain away the prediction of Israel becoming a great nation as having been written after the fact. In the seventh century B.C., Assyria, which had conquered the northern Israelite kingdom, had been overtaken by the Babylonians, and in the sixth century B.C., the Babylonians were conquered by the Persians. Again, if skeptics wish, they can suppose that Genesis 12 was written after all that had occurred (though in taking that position, they would be swimming against the tide of mainstream biblical scholarship).

However, one element of this prophecy was not fulfilled until centuries after the entire Old Testament was written, even on the most extreme view of its origins. The prediction that through Abraham all the families of the earth would be blessed was just beginning to be fulfilled when the *New* Testament era began in the early first century A.D. At that time the Jewish people had little spiritual, cultural, or intellectual influence in the known world outside its own communities. Jews were scattered throughout the Roman Empire, but many kept to themselves. Most Jews refused even to eat with Gentiles (non-Jews) and made no effort to propagate their beliefs and values to others. Smatterings of Gentiles were showing an interest in Judaism, visiting synagogues and praying to the God of Israel.

Then Christianity came along. At first, the followers of Jesus were exclusively Jewish, but about fifteen years after His death, that began to change. Some of the apostles of Jesus, especially a former rabbinical student named Paul, began actively seeking to bring Gentiles into the fold. Christianity eventually blanketed Europe, parts of Asia, and North Africa with its message that God—the same God who had spoken to

Abraham—was calling people of all nations into a relationship with Him through His Son Jesus. As Christianity grew geographically and numerically, the Jewish people also began exerting greater influence directly in the larger culture, especially in Europe. In the past half-millennium, Christianity and Judaism have come to dominate the Western Hemisphere as well.

The history of Judaism and Christianity has not, of course, been uniformly good. Many evil things have been done in the name of God, especially in medieval times but continuing even to this day. But the knowledge of God has brought many wonderful blessings as well (as we will see in the next chapter). In any case, the easy-to-understand point is this: Genesis 12 predicted that through Abraham the people of Israel would influence the faith and life of people all over the earth. At the end of the entire Old Testament period, that prediction was not even remotely coming true. However, two millennia later, the worldwide influence of the Abrahamic heritage is an indisputable fact.

We don't claim that the promise to Abraham has been completely and finally fulfilled, because we expect even more people to be touched by the message. But who could reasonably have expected two thousand years and more ago that half the population of the Earth—some three billion people now—would consider themselves believers in the God of Abraham? Yet this is what the biblical prophets confidently predicted. "The earth shall be full of the knowledge of the LORD, as the waters cover the sea" (Isaiah 11:9 KJV). In the explosive growth of belief in the Lord God throughout the world, even during the past century, we are witnessing the fulfillment of this prophecy unfolding before our very eyes.

GOOD AND BAD NEWS FOR ISRAEL

God's promise to Abraham—that those who bless him would be blessed and those who curse him would be cursed—might, if taken out of context, be viewed as an arrogant claim that God shows favoritism to Abraham's descendants, the people of Israel. However, the rest of the Bible makes it clear that God plays no favorites. According to Deuteronomy, Moses told Israel that the Lord would give them great blessings if they obeyed Him. "The LORD will establish you as a people holy to himself, as he has sworn to you, if you keep the commandments of the LORD your God, and walk in his ways" (Deuteronomy 28:9). On the other hand, if they did not obey, "all these curses" would come upon them (verse 15). The nation would be conquered by foreign nations, killed in mass numbers, and the few survivors would be scattered throughout the world (verses 16-68).

Sadly, this prophetic warning was fulfilled when Israel's divided kingdom was conquered by the Assyrians in the north and by the Babylonians in the south. Again, however, skeptics will insist that the predictions of devastation for Israel in Deuteronomy were written after the fact. Even if we grant this as a possibility for the sake of argument, the biblical prophecies concerning Israel extend far beyond the Babylonian Exile—indeed, far beyond the New Testament era.

In various places, the Bible actually predicts a new period of judgment and suffering, followed by restoration and blessing, for the Jewish people long after the Babylonian Exile. For example, Isaiah spoke of a day when "the Lord will set his hand again *the second time* to recover the remnant of his people" from the surrounding nations (Isaiah 11:11 ASV). From the seventeenth to the twentieth centuries, a growing number of Christian scholars understood this and similar prophecies to be referring to the restoration of the Jews to the land called Palestine.[1] Through a series of remarkable and tragic events—including the horror of the Holocaust—the Jews attained a restored State of Israel in the land in

1948. This is clearly not a case of an event occurring and then overzealous apologists claiming only after the fact that some obscure biblical text predicted the event. In this case, Christians claimed for centuries that the Bible predicted something that most people thought was impossible (and undesirable, given many people's hatred for the Jews).

> FREDERICK THE GREAT IS SAID ONCE TO HAVE ASKED HIS PERSONAL PHYSICIAN ZIMMERMANN WHETHER HE [ZIMMERMANN] COULD GIVE HIM AN ABSOLUTELY CERTAIN PROOF OF THE EXISTENCE OF GOD, AND TO HAVE GOT THE LACONIC REPLY "YOUR MAJESTY, THE JEWS!"
> —KARL BARTH[2]

One of the most remarkable prophecies of the second period of oppression and dispersion that ended only in the twentieth century appears in the Book of Daniel. The book tells about the visions and revelations of a Jewish man named Daniel living in Babylon during the Exile. Modern mainstream scholarship is skeptical of the apparent prophecies of the book concerning the Jews' struggles under Greek rule in the second century B.C. that culminated in the Maccabean revolt (see, for example, Daniel 8:21-22); however, it almost uniformly dates the book to that century. We could argue for a sixth-century date, but for our purposes that isn't necessary, since the prophecy in question deals with events two centuries and more *after* the Maccabean era.

The Book of Daniel predicts that a future ruler "shall destroy the city and the sanctuary" (Daniel 9:26 KJV). Now, if this prediction came through the sixth-century Daniel, it would have been made at a time when the city and the sanctuary (the Jerusalem Temple) were in ruins, some years before it was rebuilt after the Jews began returning from the Babylonian Exile. That would mean that Daniel envisioned the city and Temple being rebuilt and then destroyed *again*.

Suppose instead that we assume a second-century B.C. date for the prophecy. In that case, the city and Temple would already have been rebuilt for over three centuries. However, their second destruction still would have been about two centuries away. It was not until A.D. 70 that the second Jerusalem Temple was destroyed in the war between the Jews and the Romans (A.D. 66-73).[3]

KEY DATES PERTAINING TO DANIEL

587/586 B.C.	Babylonians destroy Solomon's Temple in Jerusalem
ca. 540 B.C.	Daniel finishes his prophecies (traditional date)
ca. 515 B.C.	Jerusalem Temple rebuilt
444 B.C.	Decree to permit the walls of Jerusalem to be rebuilt
169/168 B.C.	Antiochus IV Epiphanes defiles the Temple

ca. 164 B.C.	Late date for composition of the Book of Daniel
A.D. 33	Jesus prophesies destruction of the Temple and the "times of the Gentiles"
A.D. 50-60	Probable date of Mark, the earliest Gospel
A.D. 70	Romans destroy the Temple in Jerusalem
A.D. 1948	Israel constituted as a modern state
A.D. 1967	Israel takes control of Jerusalem

Whether one dates the Book of Daniel to the sixth or the second century B.C., his prediction that the Temple, after being rebuilt, would be destroyed again is remarkable, not merely for its prescience or advance knowledge but for its daring. During the Exile, while Solomon's Temple lay in ruins, who would ever have imagined or speculated that the Temple would be rebuilt and then destroyed again? And shortly after the Maccabees had successfully revolted against Antiochus and purified the second Temple, who would have supposed that the second Temple was nevertheless going to be destroyed? Either way, the prediction is startling in more ways than one.

According to the Gospels, Jesus also prophesied, less than forty years before it happened, that the Temple would be destroyed—specifying that its destruction would occur before His generation passed away. Speaking of the Temple, Jesus told His disciples, "Not one stone will be left upon another which will not be torn down. . . . Truly I say to you, this generation will not pass away until all these things take place" (Mark 13:2, 30 NASB). Not surprisingly, some biblical scholars date the Gospel of Mark (and the other Gospels as well) after A.D. 70. In the previous chapter, though, we gave some reasons to think that Luke—whom almost all biblical scholars think wrote after Mark and probably used Mark as a source—wrote his Gospel no later than about A.D. 60-61. But even if we suppose that all of the Gospels were written after A.D. 70, it is still most likely that Jesus did prophesy the fall of Jerusalem and the destruction of the Temple. The Gospels and the Book of Acts contain several references to Jews charging that Jesus had threatened to destroy the Temple himself (Matthew 26:61; 27:40; Mark 14:58; 15:29; Acts 6:14). This is the sort of distorted representation one might expect if Jesus had prophesied the destruction of the Temple.

One element of Jesus' prophecy as told in the Gospel of Luke is especially noteworthy. Luke reports that Jesus had warned, "Jerusalem will be trampled under foot by the Gentiles until the times of the Gentiles are fulfilled" (Luke 21:24 NASB). This statement appears to describe a period of Gentile domination over Jerusalem that could last for a very long time but that will eventually end. Of course, that is what happened. Jerusalem was dominated by Gentile powers—Roman, Christian, but especially Muslim powers—from A.D. 70 until 1967, when Israel, not quite twenty years old as a modern state, took control of Jerusalem in the Six-Day War. One could, admittedly, argue that Jewish control of Jerusalem at this point is not complete. Still, the revival of a Jewish state and of Jerusalem as at least partially under Jewish control after nineteen centuries is a remarkable turn of events. It is very reasonable to conclude that Jesus' prophecy has already been largely fulfilled and that the implied end of Gentile domination over Jerusalem is now in sight, if not in some sense already fulfilled.

BREAKING NEWS *BEFORE* IT HAPPENS!

Finally, let's go back to Daniel's prophecy that a future ruler would destroy the second Jerusalem Temple. The larger prophecy of which that prediction is a part speaks about "seventy weeks," or more literally, "seventy sevens" (Daniel 9:24-27).[4] We're going to analyze this prophecy in some detail, but be patient—the payoff is incredible.

In context the "weeks" here almost certainly refers to periods of seven years, not seven days. We know this because earlier in the passage

Daniel had been praying concerning the seventy years of Jerusalem's desolation (9:2-3). Immediately after the prophecy of the seventy weeks, Daniel mentions having fasted for "three weeks of days" (10:2-3)—evidently adding "of days" to distinguish these "weeks" from the weeks of years just mentioned.[5] In the Jewish religion, every seventh year was a kind of Sabbath year, during which the land was supposed to be left uncultivated (Leviticus 25:2-7). According to Leviticus, Moses had prophesied that the disobedient Israelites would be taken from the land by force so that the land could have its Sabbath rest (Leviticus 26:32-35, 43), a prophecy evidently understood in Daniel's day to refer to the time of the Exile.

The prophecy divides these seventy weeks of years (or 490 years) into three parts: a period of "seven weeks," or 49 years; a period of "sixty-two weeks," or 434 years; and a period of "one week," or seven years. The first period is said to correspond with a decree issued "to restore and build Jerusalem . . . with squares and moat" (Daniel 9:25). Although Cyrus in 539 B.C. had decreed that the Temple in Jerusalem should be rebuilt (2 Chronicles 36:22-23; Ezra 1:1-4), his decree did not authorize the rebuilding of Jerusalem as a city with fortifications. That decree came later from the Persian king Artaxerxes in 445 or 444 B.C. (Nehemiah 2:1-8).

To what do these multiples of seven years refer? Since the seven-year periods correspond to the cycle of sabbatical years of the Mosaic Law, we should probably view these multiples of seven years as referring to periods of more than one sabbatical cycle. This understanding is strongly supported by the fact that the first period of 49 years is a clear allusion to the Levitical requirement that every forty-nine years be followed by a fiftieth year, called the jubilee, during which various debts were to be canceled or resolved and indentured and dispossessed people restored to their families and lands (Leviticus 25:8-17). The implication for the Daniel prophecy is that the seventy weeks did not necessarily start on the very day or even in the very year of Artaxerxes' decree (although in principle, they could have started then). Rather, we should simply understand that Artaxerxes' decree fell somewhere during the first of these seven-year periods. The first 49 years appear to cover the period during which Nehemiah and Ezra worked in Jerusalem to bring about its physical restoration and spiritual reform.

The second and longest period, the 434 years, appears to follow directly after the 49 years so that together these 69 periods of seven-year sabbatical cycles cover some 483 years. We do not know with certainty what years were the sabbatical years, but the best information we have identifies the year 162 B.C. as the sabbatical year mentioned in the book of 1 Maccabees (6:49, 53-54).[6] Working backward and forward from this date, we can derive the following table representing the 69 periods of seven years.[7]

THE 69 SEVEN-YEAR SABBATICAL CYCLES

1-7	8-14	15-21	22-28	29-35	36-42	43-49	50-56	57-63	64-69
449-42	400-393	351-44	302-295	253-46	204-197	155-48	106-99	57-50	8-1
442-35	393-86	344-37	295-88	246-39	197-90	148-41	99-92	50-43	1 B.C.-A.D. 7
435-28	386-79	337-30	288-81	239-32	190-83	141-34	92-85	43-36	A.D. 7-14
428-21	379-72	330-23	281-74	232-25	183-76	134-27	85-78	36-29	14-21
421-14	372-65	323-16	274-67	225-18	176-69	127-20	78-71	29-22	21-28
414-07	365-58	316-09	267-60	218-11	169-62	120-13	71-64	22-15	28-35
407-400	358-51	309-02	260-53	211-04	162-55	113-06	64-57	15-8	

Notice that Artaxerxes' decree, dated 445 or 444 B.C., will have occurred during the first sabbatical cycle even if the dates are as much as two or three years off. The analysis is therefore not dependent upon having exact dates for these events. The sixty-ninth cycle covers the period from A.D. 28 to 35. So, what was supposed to happen then?

Daniel's prophecy states that "after the sixty-two weeks, the Messiah [literally, 'the anointed one'] will be cut off" (Daniel 9:26). Our understanding of this statement will be aided by knowing a couple of Hebrew idioms. In Hebrew usage, to be "cut off" meant to be killed—more specifically that the person had been put to death as an act of judicial punishment (Genesis 17:14; Exodus 12:15, 19; Leviticus 17:14; Numbers 15:31; etc.). It is also important to understand that the Jews counted inclusively so that "after three days," for example, was equivalent in meaning to "on the third day" (compare Matthew 20:19 with 27:63).

What Daniel was saying, then, was that during the sixty-second of those sixty-two cycles of sabbatical years—or, adding those to the first seven cycles, the sixty-ninth cycle in all—the Messiah would be put to death in an act of judicial punishment. You can probably see where we're going with this. It was during this period that Jesus conducted His public ministry of preaching and healing, and it was during this period (A.D. 28-35), in either A.D. 30 or 33, that Jesus was put to death. (Biblical scholars are divided on whether it was A.D. 30 or 33; note that for our purposes, it doesn't matter.) And why was He put to death? Well, the Roman governor had Him executed because some of the Jewish leaders told him that Jesus claimed to be the King of the Jews (Matthew 27:11, 37; Mark 15:2, 9, 12, 26; Luke 23:3, 38; John 18:33; 19:19-22). This was essentially a political equivalent for the Hebrew title Messiah ("anointed one"), which in Greek was translated as Christ (Luke 23:2).

So, it turns out that Jesus was executed for claiming to be the Messiah during the very seven-year period in which Daniel prophesied that this would occur. Again, the latest possible date for the Book of Daniel according to the most skeptical scholars is fully two centuries before Jesus' execution. This may be the most astonishing fulfilled prophecy in the Bible—especially if, as we will explain in later chapters, there is independent evidence supporting Jesus' claim to have been the Messiah.

FOR FURTHER READING

Newman, Robert C., ed. *The Evidence of Prophecy: Fulfilled Prediction as a Testimony to the Truth of Christianity.* Hatfield, Pa.: Interdisciplinary Biblical Research Institute, 1988. Collection of short, interesting essays exploring the fulfillment of various biblical prophecies.

Payne, J. Barton. *Encyclopedia of Biblical Prophecy: The Complete Guide to Scriptural Predictions and Their Fulfillment.* New York: Harper & Row, 1973. The title is no exaggeration; a massive compendium of biblical prophecies with information and analysis concerning their fulfillment.

12

The Evidence of the Bible's Profound Wisdom

DESPITE ALL CRITICISM, THE
BIBLE CONTAINS THE WISEST
COUNSEL EVER WRITTEN.

The Bible is the most often quoted book in the world—and not just on Sunday morning. Its teachings and principles are the wisest of all literature. Its laws exalt justice, according dignity to all human beings. Its insights into the human condition are both realistic and hopeful. The Bible offers sound principles concerning marriage and the family, money and possessions, character development and reconciliation. From the Ten Commandments to the Golden Rule, the Bible continues to be the greatest and wisest book ever written.

Mind you, some Christians fall woefully short of reflecting the wisdom of the Bible. Worse still, some Christians have misused the Bible to justify their foolish prejudices and conduct. The Bible has been misquoted and misinterpreted to sanction the oppression of women, the enslavement of black people, and the persecution of the Jews. It would be very easy to produce a litany of examples of biblical texts used for such purposes. The problem, though, is not with the Bible or Christianity but with the Christians who have misused the Bible to justify their behavior. The history of Christianity is largely a history of Christians struggling to catch up with the wisdom of their own Bible. Even now, the Bible is a book ahead of its time.

> *The LORD gives wisdom; from his mouth*
> *come knowledge and understanding.*
> —SOLOMON (PROVERBS 2:6)

In this chapter we can only offer a few glimpses into the profound wisdom of the Bible. Since our focus in this book is on evidence for belief in the God of the Bible, we will highlight aspects of the Bible's wisdom that are directly related to what it says about God.

CHRISTIAN FAITH:

NEITHER SUPERSTITION NOR SKEPTICISM

In matters of religion, people tend to gravitate toward the extremes of superstition and skepticism. The superstitious will believe almost anything—the kookier the better. The skeptical refuse to believe anything that doesn't fit their preconceived notions of what is possible. For the superstitious, no evidence is needed; for the skeptical, no evidence is enough. The superstitious desperately want to believe; the skeptical desperately want not to believe. The superstitious like the *National Enquirer;* the skeptical like the *Skeptical Inquirer.*

Now that we've set up the alternatives in this way, you've probably guessed that we favor a happy medium between superstition and skepticism. Well, not exactly. Yes, we think the right stance falls somewhere between these two extremes—but not necessarily in the middle. You may be surprised to learn that we think skepticism is closer to the right point of view.

The Bible is merciless in its attacks on superstition. The very first chapter of the Bible, which is often treated as if its main concerns were geophysics or biology, is primarily concerned with refuting ancient superstitious *cosmogonies,* or stories of the world's origin. These ancient cosmogonies typically represented the world as originating out of con-flicts among anthropomorphic deities. Gods and goddesses made love and war; and somehow from their primal activities, the world arose. The first chapter of Genesis repudiates such notions. One God alone creates and makes the world by His effortless decree—"Let there be light" (Genesis 1:3 KJV).

We mentioned earlier in this chapter that Genesis is not primarily concerned with geophysics and biology. While that is true, it is also true that the view of God and creation set forth in Genesis and the rest of the Bible historically encouraged the development of science. As long as a society thinks that many deities are running chaotic, indiscriminate interference with each other and with the course of events, that society is unlikely to pursue a scientific understanding of natural processes. The biblical concept of God as the intelligent Creator and Designer of the world eventually helped to create an intellectual environment in which science could flourish.

THE SCIENTIFIC QUEST FOUND FERTILE SOIL ONLY WHEN THIS FAITH IN A PERSONAL, RATIONAL CREATOR HAD TRULY PERMEATED A WHOLE

CULTURE, BEGINNING WITH THE CENTURIES OF
THE HIGH MIDDLE AGES. IT WAS THAT FAITH
WHICH PROVIDED, IN SUFFICIENT MEASURE,
CONFIDENCE IN THE RATIONALITY OF THE UNIVERSE,
TRUST IN PROGRESS, AND APPRECIATION OF THE
QUANTITATIVE METHOD, ALL INDISPENSABLE
INGREDIENTS OF THE SCIENTIFIC QUEST.

—STANLEY L. JAKI[1]

Indeed, the four individuals who did the most to pioneer modern science were pious men whose belief in God was integral to their view of science. Nicolaus Copernicus (1473-1543), by showing that the movements of the planets were more elegantly explained mathematically on the assumption that they moved around the sun rather than around the Earth, established the principle that scientific knowledge should be rooted in mathematical analysis. He was a Catholic cleric.

Galileo Galilei (1564-1642), by using the telescope to discover the moons of Jupiter and the phases of Venus and therefore proving that not all heavenly bodies move around the same center, established the principle that science must be based on empirical observation and not on dogmatic assumptions. He was a devout Catholic and wrote astute works defending his views in the light of the Bible.[2]

Johannes Kepler (1571-1630), by showing that the planets move around the sun in ellipses rather than circles, established the principle that nature's regularity cannot be assumed to conform to Greek notions of perfection. Kepler was a Lutheran and did original, ground-breaking work in biblical scholarship. He also sought to apply his research into the movements of heavenly bodies to show that those movements should not be regarded superstitiously. He was the first scientist to offer credible arguments refuting such beliefs as astrology and omens (for example, that comets are omens of impending destruction).

Isaac Newton (1642-1727), by formulating his laws of motion and gravity, established the principle that the movements of heavenly bodies and of Earth itself are governed by the same laws that govern the movements of objects here on Earth. He devoted much of his research and writing to the study of the Bible.

> WE SEE HOW GOD, LIKE A HUMAN ARCHITECT, APPROACHED THE FOUNDING OF THE WORLD ACCORDING TO ORDER AND RULE AND MEASURED EVERYTHING IN SUCH A MANNER.
>
> —JOHANNES KEPLER[5]

The polytheism of the ancient cosmogonies was part and parcel of the worldview of almost all ancient societies. Virtually everyone believed, as Thomas Cahill puts it, "in many (and conflicting) gods and godlets—bad-tempered forces of nature and the cosmos who could be temporarily appeased by just the right rites and rigmarole."[4] The biblical idea that one God alone created and ruled over the cosmos swept away a multitude of superstitious worries. If you're a monotheist, you don't worry about inquiring whenever you enter a different tribe's territory as to what gods they worship and how you can stay on their good side. The God of the Bible gives us everything and needs nothing; His commands are not arbitrary rules imposed as tests of loyalty but principles that reflect the way that He designed us.

The God who made the world and all things in it, since He is Lord of heaven and earth, does not dwell in temples made with hands; nor is He served by human hands, as though He needed anything, since He Himself gives to all people life and breath and all things; and He made from one man every nation of mankind to live on all the face of the earth.

—PAUL (ACTS 17:24-26 NASB)

Of course the Bible, especially the Old Testament, includes the use of religious rites as familiar points of reference for the ancient Israelites to relate to the Lord their God. But throughout the Bible, one finds that God is working to wean His people from dependence on such external observances. Isaiah told the Israelites of his day, "'What are your multiplied sacrifices to Me?' says the Lord. 'I have had enough of burnt offerings of rams and the fat of fed cattle; and I take no pleasure in the blood of bulls, lambs or goats'" (Isaiah 1:11 NASB). Isaiah went on to tell his people that what God wanted was right behavior: "Cease to do evil, learn to do good; seek justice, reprove the ruthless, defend the orphan, plead for the widow" (verses 16-17 NASB). Biblical religion was always principally about doing right, not doing rites.

Almost eight centuries later, Jesus signaled the end of ritual-centered religion. Speaking to a Samaritan woman who asked Jesus whether God should be worshiped on Mount Gerizim in Samaria or Mount Zion (Jerusalem) in Judea, Jesus answered her: "Believe me, the time is coming when it will no longer matter whether you worship the Father here or in Jerusalem. . . . True worshipers will worship the Father in spirit and in truth" (John 4:21, 23 NLT). Sadly, a significant factor in the centuries-old conflict in the Middle East, especially between Jews and Muslims but to some extent also involving some Christian groups, is the belief that Jerusalem is a holy place that must be controlled by the right religion. To listen to Jesus, though, Jerusalem is no holier than any other place. God meets His people wherever they are, be it Jerusalem, Joplin, or Johannesburg.

The Bible, then, while it encourages faith in God, discourages superstitious beliefs and practices—not only those of other religions but those that manifest themselves among believers in the God of the Bible. Far from rubber-stamping the prejudices and superstitions of the people who produced it, the Bible challenged the religious assumptions of the Israelite people to the core and continues to challenge believers in God from all nations and cultures.

THE BIBLE: THE ORIGINAL CHARTER OF HUMAN RIGHTS

For people who believe in many gods, it is natural also to believe that some people are closer to being gods than others. It is not surprising, then, that many ancient cultures viewed their king (and his family) as divine. From the Pharaohs of ancient Egypt to the early Roman emperors—some of whom called themselves Lord and God—

rulers often cemented their hold on power by claiming to be gods. Such arrogant claims, backed up of course with military power, were the common pretext for oppression.

One of the implications of the biblical view of God is that all such claims to divinity by mortal rulers should be viewed as bogus. The king is no more a god than the peasant. Nero was no more a god than his dog was. In Psalm 82, after calling unjust judges (in Israel!) "gods"—evidently in irony—the Psalmist warns them: "Nevertheless, you shall die like men, and fall like any prince" (see verses 6-7). He then cries out to God to pass that judgment: "Arise, O God, judge the earth!" (verse 8). The Psalmist is asking, in effect, "Will the real God please stand up?" Only the Lord, the Creator of all things, to whom belongs "all the nations" (verse 8), is truly God and is qualified to judge the earth.

In place of the prevailing notion in ancient civilization of the deification of the king, the Bible affirms not only that the Lord alone is God but also that all human beings—male and female—are created in God's "image" (Genesis 1:26-27). In the immediate context of that statement, we are also told that human beings were created to exercise "dominion" over the rest of the living things on the earth (verse 28). In ancient religious thinking, the king (such as the pharaoh) was sometimes regarded as the human image or manifestation of a god. The statement in Genesis, then, meant that the image of the one true God was to be found not exclusively in the king but in all human beings.

The implications (of the image of God being reflected in all human beings) for human relationships are many and profound. If we are all created in God's image and are all to exercise dominion, then any ruler or state's authority is properly *limited*. Totalitarianism, the autocratic rule of despots, or any other form of government that makes the civil authorities unaccountable to the rest of the people is incompatible with the biblical view of human dignity. Any government that oppresses its people is an affront to God and to His purpose in creating human beings.

What a Few American Leaders
Have Said about the Bible

WE HAVE STAKED THE WHOLE FUTURE OF AMERICAN CIVILIZATION, NOT UPON THE POWER OF GOVERNMENT, FAR FROM IT. WE HAVE STAKED THE FUTURE OF ALL OF OUR POLITICAL INSTITUTIONS UPON THE CAPACITY OF MANKIND OF SELF-GOVERNMENT; UPON THE CAPACITY OF EACH AND ALL OF US TO GOVERN OURSELVES, TO CONTROL

OURSELVES, TO SUSTAIN OURSELVES ACCORDING TO THE TEN COMMANDMENTS OF GOD.
—JAMES MADISON

CAN THE LIBERTIES OF A NATION BE THOUGHT SECURE WHEN WE HAVE REMOVED THEIR ONLY FIRM BASIS, A CONVICTION IN THE MINDS OF THE PEOPLE THAT THESE LIBERTIES ARE THE GIFT OF GOD?
—THOMAS JEFFERSON

IF WE ABIDE BY THE PRINCIPLES TAUGHT IN THE BIBLE, OUR COUNTRY WILL GO ON PROSPERING AND TO PROSPER; BUT IF WE AND OUR POSTERITY NEGLECT ITS INSTRUCTIONS AND AUTHORITY, NO MAN CAN TELL HOW SUDDEN A CATASTROPHE MAY OVERWHELM US AND BURY ALL OUR GLORY IN PROFOUND OBSCURITY.
—DANIEL WEBSTER

I BELIEVE THE BIBLE IS THE BEST GIFT GOD HAS EVER GIVEN TO MAN. ALL THE GOOD FROM THE SAVIOUR OF THE WORLD IS COMMUNICATED TO US THROUGH THIS BOOK.
—ABRAHAM LINCOLN

THE BIBLE IS THE SHEET ANCHOR OF OUR LIBERTIES.
—ULYSSES S. GRANT

Let's not miss some of the specific implications for human relationships in society that the biblical view of God and of human beings as God's image entails. We have already mentioned that Genesis 1 specifically says that "male and female" were created in God's image. It has taken Jews and Christians about two thousand years since the time of Jesus to catch up with this Old Testament truth, and still we're not really done. Frankly, we'd be really embarrassed if the Bible said that women were not created in God's image or if the Bible had spoken of women as spiritually inferior and unworthy. But it doesn't. Not that such ideas weren't around in biblical times! One thinks, for example, of the very last line of the so-called Gospel of Thomas, a fictitious gospel that claims to present sayings of Jesus. The last of these sayings has Jesus asserting that a woman can become worthy to enter God's kingdom if she makes herself male: "Every woman who will make herself male will enter the kingdom of heaven" (Gospel of Thomas 114).[5] Such a statement would not have been at all shocking in Jesus' day, though the biblical Gospels reveal a Jesus who would never have said such a thing. What is surprising is that the Bible never teaches such ideas about women. Instead, it holds up an elevated view of women, especially in the teaching and ministry of Jesus and His apostle Paul.

The biblical view of the image of God as found in all people also extends to people of all races or ethnicities. One of the more remarkable silences of the Bible is its lack of any discussion or comment about differences between people of varying skin colors. We are often asked what the Bible says about the origin of the different races. Our answer, frankly, is this: nothing. Students of the Bible have their guesses, some better than others, but the Bible doesn't address the question—evidently because it doesn't matter.

What the Bible does say is that people of all races and colors come from the same origin. According to Paul, God "made from one man every nation of mankind to live on all the face of the earth" (Acts 17:26 NASB). This doctrine goes back to Genesis, which teaches that all human beings are descended from Adam and Eve—and in fact that we are all descended from Noah (Genesis 1:26-27; 3:20; 6:17-18; 7:23; 10:1-32).

Racism, then, of any kind is at odds with the Bible. That includes attitudes of hostility toward the Jews, a besetting sin of much of Christianity for most of its history. Jesus and His apostles were Jewish (see, for example, John 4:9). The Gospel of John reports Jesus as having stated that "salvation is from the Jews" (John 4:22 ASV). In other words, it was God's plan, as we saw in the previous chapter, to bring the blessings of a restored relationship with God to all people through Abraham's descendants, the Jews (Genesis 12:1-3). Even when, as happened during the first century, the Jewish establishment was vehemently opposed to the Christian movement, the apostle Paul (himself Jewish) insisted that the Jews were to be regarded as "beloved" (Romans 11:28).

The last book of the Bible, the Book of Revelation, includes stirring visions of people singing before God's throne—people who come, in fulfillment of God's promise to Abraham, "from every tribe and tongue and people and nation" (Revelation 5:9; see also 7:9; 14:6). This isn't just a picture of God's people at the end of history. It's also a picture of what God's people should be becoming now and what they have already largely become (though far from perfect). Again, it's taken us a long time to catch up with the Bible, and we're still not there 100 percent. But that's just what we would expect if the Bible was divinely inspired: a revelation whose values would transcend those of its own era, one that would continually challenge God's people to discover their own prejudices and shortcomings.

> TO MOSES WE OWE THE EMERGENCE OF
> HIGHER RELIGIOUS LIFE AND MORAL
> CULTURE IN WESTERN CIVILIZATION.
> —WILLIAM FOXWELL ALBRIGHT[6]

The Bible's view of human beings also has implications for socio-economic relationships. In this regard the Bible maintains a fine line. On the one hand, the Bible does not call for violent or disruptive revolt against societies that marginalize or oppress people. Moses led the Israelite slaves out of Egypt and back to their own land; he did not lead an armed revolt against the Egyptian government. Jesus did not support the Zealots—a Jewish movement that called for the violent overthrow of Roman rule in Judea.

On the other hand, the Bible harshly condemns economic injustice and warns of God's judgment (often through other aggressive nations) against nations (even and especially Israel!) that do not correct such injustice. Thus Amos, for example, warned Israel that the rich who "impose heavy rent on the poor and exact a tribute of grain from them" will find themselves without homes or property if they do not change their ways (Amos 5:11 NASB). Paul, while not telling slaveowners that they had to free their slaves, encouraged slaves to obtain their freedom if they could—a clear signal to their Christian masters to accommodate such efforts (1 Corinthians 7:21-23). The biblical ideal of the brother-hood of all human beings—a brotherhood that the New Testament emphasizes is realized through Jesus—eventually led nations dominated by Christian teaching and values to abolish slavery and to lead the way in working to abolish slavery worldwide.

So, in its teaching about men and women, about people of different ethnicity and color, and about people of different economic status or position, the Bible shows itself to be far more enlightened, not only than the culture of its day but also in comparison to most of civilization since it was written. We're still working to realize Paul's breathtaking vision: "There is neither Jew nor Greek, there is neither slave nor free, there is neither male nor female; for you are all one in Christ Jesus" (Galatians 3:28).

FOR FURTHER READING

Boa, Kenneth D., and Robert M. Bowman Jr. *An Unchanging Faith in a Changing World: Understanding and Responding to Issues that Christians Face Today.* Nashville: Thomas Nelson, Oliver, 1997. Includes chapters detailing and defending the biblical view of science, culture, and values.

Kantzer, Kenneth S., and Carl F. H. Henry, eds. *Evangelical Affirmations.* Grand Rapids: Zondervan—Academic Books, 1990. A collection of essays expounding on the social and cultural implications of biblical faith.

13

The Evidence of Jesus' Life

> ## NO ONE CAN AFFORD TO IGNORE JESUS, THE MOST COMPELLING PERSON IN HISTORY.

Our purpose in this book is not merely to persuade you that God exists, as important as that truth is. We want you to know that the God who created the universe has lovingly reached down to us in a very concrete and tangible way. As astonishing as it seems, we are convinced that He has made himself known in the man called Jesus of Nazareth.

Consider Jesus.

—HEBREWS 3:1

That Jesus is the most influential person in human history is easily shown. Even someone with no interest in becoming a Christian cannot reasonably deny the importance of understanding who this most controversial of men was. More than half the people of the world regard Him as at least a major prophet of their religion, if not more. Christianity, the largest world religion, looks to Jesus as its founder, primary teacher, and, traditionally at least, its God and Savior. Islam, the second largest world religion, regards Jesus as a holy prophet of Allah. Obviously, no one can hope to understand the world today who does not understand Christianity and Islam.

The history of Western civilization during the past two millennia is largely the history of how people have viewed Jesus and how their view of Him shaped the rest of their lives. Jaraslov Pelikan, a Yale historian, has sketched this history in his fascinating book *Jesus through the Centuries.*[1] During His own lifetime, Jesus was widely regarded in His own culture as a rabbi or a prophet, both categories familiar to His Jewish contemporaries. Yet His immediate followers, all of whom were Jewish, proclaimed that He was more than these—and more than a man: He was the Son of God.

As belief in Jesus spread to non-Jewish people throughout the Mediterranean region, Christians sought to relate to Jesus as the ideal human being as well as the divine Son of God. In their sufferings, especially during the first three centuries of church history, Christians saw Jesus as someone who both sympathized with their plight because of His own suffering and promised them vindication in His future glorious return in judgment. During the Middle Ages, believers saw Jesus as both the cosmic King of Kings and as the perfect example of detachment from the world expressed in monasticism.

On the eve of the Renaissance, Francis of Assisi and Thomas à Kempis sought to imitate Jesus in the simplicity and purity of His life. The view of Martin Luther and John Calvin, the Protestant Reformers, of Jesus as the only head of the Church and the sole object of Christian faith laid the groundwork for the modern separation of church and state and the development of representative democracy in almost every predominantly Protestant country. Jesus' association in the Gospels with the poor and downtrodden inspired the abolition of slavery throughout most of the world in the nineteenth century and the civil disobedience movements of Gandhi in India and of Martin Luther King in the United States.

Whatever one thinks of Jesus—or of His followers, who have often failed to live up to the teaching and example of Jesus—one cannot afford to ignore Him.

> REGARDLESS OF WHAT ANYONE MAY PERSONALLY
> THINK OR BELIEVE ABOUT HIM, JESUS OF
> NAZARETH HAS BEEN THE DOMINANT FIGURE IN
> THE HISTORY OF WESTERN CULTURE FOR ALMOST
> TWENTY CENTURIES. . . . IT IS FROM HIS BIRTH THAT
> MOST OF THE HUMAN RACE DATES ITS CALENDARS,
> IT IS BY HIS NAME THAT MILLIONS CURSE AND
> IN HIS NAME THAT MILLIONS PRAY.
>
> —JARASLOV PELIKAN[2]

DID JESUS EXIST?

Was Jesus a real human being? While it is possible to find a few skeptical scholars who theorize that Jesus may never have existed, this view is about as credible as the opinions that the earth is a flat disk or that little green men live on the far side of Mars. At least three virtually irrefutable reasons guarantee that Jesus was indeed a real, historical person.

First, the undisputed epistles of Paul clearly testify to the fact that Jesus was a real human being. These epistles were written between A.D. 48/49 and A.D. 57/58, or about fifteen to twenty-five years after Jesus' death. Paul was personally acquainted with "James, the Lord's brother" (Galatians 1:19) and at least one other brother of Jesus (1 Corinthians 9:5). Presumably Jesus' brothers knew that He was a real person! Paul also knew Peter, one of Jesus' original twelve disciples (Galatians 1:18). Paul affirmed that Jesus was "born of a woman" (Galatians 4:4) and that He was a descendant of David (Romans 1:3). He knew that Jesus was betrayed, and he knew that on the night it happened, Jesus had instituted the ritual with bread and wine celebrated by Christians worldwide (1 Corinthians 11:23-25). He knew that Christ was put to death by crucifixion (1 Corinthians 1:23). He affirmed that Christ was buried following His death (1 Corinthians 15:4). Keep in mind that when Paul wrote about Jesus having all of these human experiences, none of the Gospels had been written yet. Thus, his epistles constitute independent evidence to these historical facts about Jesus.

Second, we have independent sources in and underlying the Gospels that agree as to the existence of Jesus and that agree concerning various basic facts about His person. Biblical scholars almost universally regard the Book of Mark as the first Gospel written. A large body of material common to Matthew and Luke's Gospels seems to stem from another source. Luke states at the beginning of his Gospel that various accounts had been written about Jesus (Luke 1:1-4). These Gospel sources agree with one another—and with Paul on the points mentioned earlier—as to Jesus' historical existence and various mundane facts about His life. And don't forget that there is evidence, as we saw in chapter 10, that the Gospel writers intended to give accurate historical information about Jesus (see again Luke 1:1-4; also John 19:35; 21:24-25).

> ## THE HISTORICITY OF CHRIST IS AS AXIOMATIC FOR AN UNBIASED HISTORIAN AS THE HISTORICITY OF JULIUS CAESAR.
> —F. F. BRUCE[3]

The two points mentioned so far put the burden of proof squarely on the skeptic to provide compelling evidence against the historical existence of Jesus. We may grant that the burden of proof rests on the believer to defend, say, the remarkable historical claims that Jesus was born of a virgin and rose bodily from the grave. It is not unreasonable for skeptics to ask for evidence in support of such controversial and extraordinary claims. On the question of whether Jesus was a real historical figure, on the other hand, the burden of proof rests on the skeptic to show why the Bible's mundane claims about Jesus should be doubted. That Jesus was a Jew, that His father Joseph was a carpenter, that He was related to John the Baptist, that He taught disciples and preached to crowds, and that He was executed by crucifixion at the order of the procurator Pontius Pilate ought

to be considered facts unless proved otherwise.

> A CHARACTER SO ORIGINAL, SO COMPLETE,
> SO UNIFORMLY CONSISTENT, SO PERFECT, SO
> HUMAN AND YET SO HIGH ABOVE ALL HUMAN
> GREATNESS, CAN BE NEITHER A FRAUD NOR
> A FICTION. . . . IT WOULD TAKE MORE
> THAN A JESUS TO INVENT A JESUS.
>
> —PHILIP SCHAFF[*]

A third consideration puts all reasonable doubt to rest. A significant

measure of what the Gospels say about Jesus would have embarrassed or

troubled most people in the early Church. These difficult elements in

the Gospels can only realistically be explained on the assumption

(which is in any case well founded, as we have seen) that Jesus really

existed. For example, the Gospels report Jesus saying things that the

Church has always struggled to understand, such as his rebuke to Peter,

"Get behind me, Satan!" (Matthew 16:23; Mark 8:33) or His statement,

"The poor you always have with you" (John 12:8). Jesus' well-known

friendship with prostitutes is just one of many examples we could give

of behaviors that the Gospels attribute to Jesus that are very unlikely to

have been pious fictions. The idea that Jesus had been crucified—a humiliating, shameful form of execution reserved by the Romans mainly for traitors and runaway slaves—was nothing short of scandalous (1 Corinthians 1:23-24).[5]

Perhaps through creative use of the imagination, skeptics may be able to explain away a few such elements of the Gospel accounts as fictions about an imaginary person. However, no reasonable theory postulating that Jesus never existed can hope to explain away all of these aspects of the New Testament portrayal of Jesus. It really ought to be considered beyond reasonable doubt that the best and most reasonable explanation for the facts is that Jesus was a real, historical person.

Some Indisputable Facts about Jesus[6]

1. He was born about 4 B.C.
2. He was Jewish.
3. He grew up in Nazareth in Galilee.
4. His ministry was at first closely associated with that of John the Baptist.
5. He preached and taught in various places in Galilee.
6. He called disciples who went with Him during His ministry.
7. He went to Jerusalem for the Passover around A.D. 30 or so.
8. He caused a disturbance in the temple area concerning the money changers.
9. He was executed by crucifixion on the order of the Roman procurator, Pontius Pilate.
10. His disciples soon after His death began saying that He had risen from the dead.

A Most Compelling Person

One of the great lessons of the nineteenth-century "quest for the historical Jesus," as Albert Schweitzer called it, is that Jesus refuses to fit anyone's stereotype. The philosophers wanted to make Jesus into a philosopher. The poets wanted to make Jesus into a poet. The political revolutionaries wanted to make Jesus into a political revolutionary. You get the idea. There is enough truth in these and the many other portraits that have been painted of Jesus for them to continue to be entertained by some even to this day. But all such revisionist attempts to redefine Jesus according to some modern mold are doomed to failure.

Jesus transcended the categories, the pigeonholes into which people were placed, in His own day as well. Theologically, He had more in common with the Pharisees—whose emphasis on the rabbinical study of the Law of Moses became normative for Judaism after the destruction of the Temple in A.D. 70—than with the other Jewish groupings of that time. But Jesus clearly was not a Pharisee. Throughout His public ministry, religious leaders tried to get Jesus to commit himself to a particular cause or party line so that they could tar Him with the appropriate brush. He slipped through their grip every time.

Probably the most heated controversy of Jesus' day centered on how pious Jewish men should respond to the occupation of their land by the Roman Empire. On one side of this issue were the Herodians (partisans of the royal family of Herod, which was kept in power by Rome) and the Sadducees (whose power base centered on the Temple), who favored accommodation with the Romans. On the other side were the Zealots and like-minded people, including many but not all Pharisees, who urged resistance and even violent revolution to rid the land of the Romans' polluting presence.

In one famous incident toward the end of Jesus' life, some Pharisees and Herodians—two groups who were generally on opposite sides of the controversy over taxes—tried to get Jesus to incriminate himself in the matter one way or the other. "Is it lawful to pay taxes to Caesar, or not? Should we pay them, or should we not?" (Mark 12:14-15). This was a pretty clever attempt to trap Jesus on the horns of a political dilemma. If Jesus said that Jews should pay the tax to Caesar, His answer would be construed as capitulating to the foreign, pagan enemy. If, on the other hand, Jesus said that the Jews should not pay the tax to Caesar, His answer would be reported to the Roman authorities as treasonous.

Jesus' response was masterful. He asked them to show Him the coin used for the tax. Turns out they had the coin on hand—suggesting that at least one of them had already answered the question for himself. Jesus asked them whose image and name were on the coin. "Caesar's," they replied. "Render to Caesar the things that are Caesar's," He answered them, "and to God the things that are God's" (Mark 12:17). His point was something like this: People who have no trouble accepting payment in Roman coins ought not to have any objection to letting Caesar have some of his money back; but human beings, who bear God's image and belong to Him, ought to give themselves wholly to God.

> IF WE SEE SOMEONE BEHAVING POMPOUSLY AND ARROGANTLY, WE SOMETIMES SAY, "HE THINKS HE'S GOD ALMIGHTY." BUT THAT'S A GROSS SLUR ON GOD. CHRISTIANITY FOCUSES ON A YOUNG JEW TELLING STORIES ABOUT THE KINGDOM OF GOD, HEALING THE SICK, CONFRONTING THE POWERFUL, DYING UNDER THE WEIGHT OF THE WORLD'S PAIN, AND RISING AGAIN HAVING DEFEATED DEATH ITSELF; AND CHRISTIANITY SAYS: "THAT'S WHAT IT MEANS TO BE GOD."
> —TOM WRIGHT[7]

While Jesus refused to allow himself to become embroiled in the political controversies of the day, He was not shy about challenging the status quo. We see this in His behavior toward women. Jesus showed sensitivity, compassion, and respect for women in ways very much out of character for Jewish men of his day (and for Jewish and Christian men for most of history since Jesus, to be candid!). Let's consider a few examples from the Gospel of Luke.[8]

On one occasion Jesus allowed an immoral woman—very possibly a prostitute—to wash His feet with her tears and dry them with her hair, after which He forgave her sins (Luke 7:36-50). Jesus healed a woman on the Sabbath who had been crippled for eighteen years; His kindness to her stands in sharp contrast to the uncaring synagogue ruler who objected to Jesus "working" on the Sabbath. Jesus responded to this objection in part by pointing out that the woman was "a daughter of Abraham"—suggesting that Abraham's daughters, no less than his sons, are offered the blessings of the kingdom of God (13:10-17). Jesus commended the poor widow who gave "two copper coins" because she gave everything she had while the rich gave only what they did not need (21:1-4). No wonder that various women followed Jesus and supported His ministry financially (8:1-3). Jesus even defended Mary of Bethany when she sat at His feet—the traditional place for students learning from their rabbi, a role reserved in that culture for men only—over her sister Martha's objection that she should have kept to the traditional women's role of meal preparations and the like (10:38-42).

If God were to make himself known supremely and definitively in one human being, this is what He would be like. Jesus is a compelling reason to believe in God because He is such a compelling person. He was smart, funny, and passionate. His teachings enthralled, inspired, and irritated people. He catches people off guard today just as much as He did two thousand years ago. Almost everyone wants to claim to be on Jesus' side, but if we're honest we have to wonder if we, too, might have called for His execution if He had lived in our generation. Jesus is the One person in history about whom almost everyone has a strong opinion. You owe it to yourself to find out who He really was.

FOR FURTHER READING

Wilkins, Michael, ed. *Jesus under Fire: Crucial Questions about Jesus.* Grand Rapids: Zondervan, 1995. Excellent collection of essays documenting the evidence for the reliability of the New Testament historical claims about Jesus.

Wright, Tom. *The Original Jesus: The Life and Vision of a Revolutionary.* Grand Rapids: Eerdmans, 1996. Popular-level book by a renowned historical Jesus scholar, offering a fresh look at the life and teachings of Jesus.

14

THE EVIDENCE OF JESUS' CLAIMS

> BY CLAIMING TO BE GOD, JESUS
> LEFT US NO ROOM TO VIEW HIM AS
> JUST A GREAT TEACHER.

Most people have no trouble admitting that Jesus existed or that He was a great man. In fact, it is difficult to find anyone with the nerve to say anything critical of Jesus. Yet most people in the world are not Christians. Their attitude toward Jesus is similar to the attitude most people have toward the other founders of the world's great religions, such as Muhammad, Gautama the Buddha, or Moses. They think of Jesus, as they think of these other men, as a great religious teacher. From that starting point, people naturally draw the conclusion that Jesus is one of several great teachers that one might reasonably choose to follow.

> HOW WOULD TELLING PEOPLE TO BE NICE
> TO ONE ANOTHER GET A MAN CRUCIFIED?
> WHAT GOVERNMENT WOULD CRUCIFY
> MISTER ROGERS OR CAPTAIN KANGAROO?
> —PHILIP YANCEY[1]

WHAT JESUS CLAIMED

Contrary to the popular view that Jesus was simply one of many great religious teachers, Jesus made some startling, even disturbing, claims about himself. In fact, Jesus made the faith that He taught center *on himself* rather than on some moral or social program or set of doctrines. The core issue that Jesus raised in His teaching and that is at the heart of the entire New Testament is this: *Who is Jesus?*

> *But who do you say that I am?*
> —JESUS (MARK 8:29)

A few examples from the Gospels will illustrate the point. Early in His ministry, Jesus told a paralyzed man, "Your sins are forgiven." This is really an audacious thing for Jesus to have said to someone who had never even met Jesus. It's fine to forgive someone for sins they commit against you; it's quite another thing to forgive sins committed against someone else. In short, Jesus was acting as though all of the man's sins were sins *committed against Jesus*. Some scribes who overheard asked a natural question: "Who can forgive sins but God alone?" Jesus then showed He had such authority by healing the man (Mark 2:1-12; see also Luke 7:47-50).

A climactic moment in Jesus' ministry came when He asked His disciples, "Who do people say that I am?" (Mark 8:27 NASB). The people were engaged in considerable speculation on this very question as a result of Jesus' miracles. Some thought He was John the Baptist (who had been beheaded early in Jesus' ministry) raised from the dead. Others thought he was Elijah or one of the other Old Testament prophets (Mark 6:14-16; 8:27-28). Then Jesus asked the more pressing question: "But who do *you* say that I am?" When Peter answered, "You are the Christ," Jesus told them not to tell people about him yet (Mark 8:29-30 NASB, emphasis added by authors). Most of the people were simply not ready to hear who He was.

The popular Jewish conception of the Christ, or Messiah, was that he would restore the Davidic kingdom by force and run the Romans out of the Promised Land. But Jesus did not fit that mold. A few days before His death, Jesus pointed out that David himself called the Messiah "Lord" (Psalm 110:1). Jesus then posed a question that stumped everyone: How could David call his own descendant "Lord"? (Mark 12:35-37). It is only our cultural distance from the first-century Jews that keeps us from feeling shocked at such an argument. Jesus was claiming to be greater than His father David! He was claiming to be David's *Lord*.

Everywhere we look in the Gospels, Jesus speaks in a way that places himself above all of humanity. For example, Jesus routinely referred to God as "my Father." Two thousand years of Christianity has made it difficult for some of us to be surprised by this, but it was shocking to the Jews of Jesus' day. The high priest condemned Jesus as a blasphemer for claiming to be God's "Son" (Mark 14:61-64; John 19:7). Jesus claimed that as "the Son," He alone could reveal "the Father" to others (Matthew 11:27; Luke 10:22). Imagine, someone claiming that no one can know God except through Him!

> JESUS PRESENTED HIMSELF THROUGHOUT
> THE GOSPELS, NOT FIRST AS A PROPHET,
> BUT AS THE OBJECT OF PROPHECY.
> —GEORGE CAREY[2]

Jesus' staggering claims for himself make it impossible to categorize Him as one of many great religious teachers. They amount to an "all or nothing" proposition: either we accept Him as God's divine Son and our Lord, Savior, and Judge, or we reject him. As C. S. Lewis noted, Jesus did not leave open to us a moderate assessment:

A man who was merely a man and said the sort of things Jesus said would not be a great moral teacher. He would either be a lunatic—on a level with the man who says he is a poached egg—or else he would be the Devil of Hell. You must make your choice. Either this man was, and is, the Son of God: or else a madman or something worse. You can shut Him up for a fool, you can spit at Him and kill Him as a demon; or you can fall at His feet and call Him Lord and God. But let us not come with any patronizing nonsense about His being a great human teacher. He has not left that open to us. He did not intend to.[3]

WAS JESUS A LIAR? A LUNATIC?

Given what we find Jesus saying in the Gospels, there are only a limited number of conclusions one can draw about what to make of Jesus. Let's take them one at a time.

First, one might conclude that Jesus did say these things and that they do amount to divine claims but that He was wrong. Unfortunately, as C. S. Lewis points out above, if Jesus falsely claimed to be God's Son, His error cannot be dismissed as a minor mistake. We would have to conclude that He was lying or deranged.

To our knowledge no one in history has ever proposed that Jesus was consciously lying about being divine. Apparently it's too obvious to everyone that Jesus would not have lied about being God's Son all the way to the cross. And this lie would be the worst possible lie one could tell about oneself. We're not talking about someone embellishing his résumé!

	Great, wise persons	All other persons
Persons who claim to be the only, eternal Son of God	Jesus	A few mentally insane
Persons who do not claim to be the only, eternal Son of God	Moses, Buddha, Muhammad . . .	Vast majority of people

Could Jesus have been out of His mind? This theory also has few if any takers today. The clarity, wisdom, and power of His words make such an assessment impossible. As C. S. Lewis noted, "The discrepancy between the depth and sanity of His moral teaching and the rampant megalomania which must lie behind His theological teaching unless He is indeed God has never been satisfactorily explained."[4]

WAS THE DIVINE JESUS A LEGEND?

Most people who have thought about the matter and who do not want to believe that Jesus is God argue that Jesus never claimed to be God. Most often, they take the position that Jesus did not make the divine claims reported in the Gospels. Those claims are said to have been legendary inventions of the early Church.

This theory founders on one simple fact: the early Christians all accepted the Jewish God. In the Old Testament, and in Judaism throughout its history, there is no more sacred truth than this: "Hear, O Israel! The LORD is our God, the LORD is one! You shall love the LORD your God with all your heart and with all your soul and with all your might" (Deuteronomy 6:4-5 NASB). This text is known in Judaism as the *Shema*

(Hebrew for "Hear") and is the closest thing to a creed in Judaism. In this verse and throughout the Old Testament, a clear line was drawn between the LORD God as the Creator and everything else, including all human beings, as his creation. It was completely unacceptable and unthinkable for Jews to elevate a mere man, no matter how great he was, to the level of deity.

The New Testament assumes and builds on the Jewish concept of God. In all of the Gospels, Jesus explicitly affirms that there is only one God and even identifies the *Shema* as the greatest commandment (Matthew 22:36-38; Mark 12:28-30; Luke 10:25-28; John 17:3). He quotes from the Old Testament and affirms the divine inspiration and unerring truth of the Scriptures (see, for example, Matthew 5:17-18; Mark 7:6-13; Luke 20:41-44; John 5:39-47). The rest of the New Testament is just as steeped in Jewish faith and idiom. The belief in one true God distinct from all creation is affirmed explicitly in the writings of Paul (Romans 3:29-30), James (James 2:19), and John (1 John 5:20-21) and is presupposed everywhere else.

The idea that divinity was ascribed to Jesus by His followers rather than claimed by Jesus himself requires another assumption: that belief in Jesus' deity arose as Christianity developed over time. Jesus' original

THE EVIDENCE OF JESUS' CLAIMS

Jewish followers, in this view, saw Him as an exalted human being; it was Gentile Christians of a subsequent generation who went further and ascribed deity to Jesus. In other words, the Christian view of Jesus as God incarnate is said to be the product of legends that developed long after Jesus and His original followers were gone. But this assumption also falls under the weight of the facts. Not only are the New Testament writings thoroughly Jewish in their theological and religious roots, but there is no evidence of development from belief in an exalted human Jesus to belief in a divine Jesus. The earliest parts of the Gospels and of the rest of the New Testament all support belief in Jesus as deity.

The Gospel of Mark is almost universally regarded in modern biblical scholarship as the earliest of the four Gospels, which is why we drew extensively from Mark in documenting Jesus' extraordinary claims. Mark's gospel is usually dated sometime in the 60s, or roughly thirty years after Jesus' death. The Jesus of Mark teaches with divine authority (Mark 1:22), forgives sins (Mark 2:1-12), commands the forces of nature (Mark 4:35-41), and claims to be God's Son and David's Lord (Mark 12:35-37; 13:32; 14:61-62).

Paul's writings are generally regarded as the earliest New Testament writings (unless one accepts an early date for the epistle of James). Most of his epistles are dated in the 50s, roughly fifteen to twenty-five years after Jesus' death. But Paul also strongly affirms that Jesus was divine. Paul's Jesus is the Son whom God sent into the world as a man for our redemption (Romans 8:3; Galatians 4:4-5). He has "the name which is above every name," that is, the name of the Lord (Philippians 2:9-11). He is, in fact, the Lord of the Old Testament, the One on whom everyone may call for salvation (Romans 10:9-13, quoting Joel 2:32). And Paul makes such statements about Jesus with no indication that he thought his Christian readers would be surprised or puzzled by them. This means that the belief in Jesus as the divine Son of God was already standard fare in churches from Galatia (in modern Turkey) to Rome within two decades of Jesus' death.

The theory that Jesus' claims to deity were the stuff of later legend, then, does not stand up to scrutiny. There is no reasonable way to get around the fact that He did make such astonishing claims to be the universal Lord, Savior, and Judge of mankind.

WAS JESUS THE LOCAL LAMA?

There is one other alternative explanation left for Jesus' extraordinary claims, which we feel compelled to mention because of its recent

THE EVIDENCE OF JESUS' CLAIMS

rise in popularity. There are now some people who are prepared to admit that He said those things (or at least some of those things) but argue that He didn't mean them in the exclusive, "narrow" way that Christians take them. Those who choose this alternative typically prefer to view Jesus' statements as esoteric, mystical expressions. The mystical reconstruction of Jesus views Him as a Hindu guru from Galilee, a kind of Buddhist teacher of enlightenment for the West. Yes, these interpreters of Jesus admit that He did claim to be God; but then, in their view, we're *all* God.

The Gospels flatly contradict such conceptions of Jesus. There is no trace in Jesus' teachings of the ideas most fundamental to Eastern mysticism, such as the underlying divinity in all things. He was, rather, a Scripture-quoting Jewish man whose claims are just as scandalous to the Eastern or New Age mindset as they were in His own Jewish culture. As we have seen, He assumed the Jewish, Old Testament view of God as the sole Creator of everything else and the Lord to whom all creatures are accountable. He affirmed that salvation came to the world through the Jews (John 4:22).

> ## TO CLASSIFY JESUS AS A GURU IS AS ACCURATE AS CLASSIFYING MARX AS A CAPITALIST.
> —PETER KREEFT AND RONALD TACELLI[*]

Jesus' claims for himself likewise will not fit into a mystical context. He forgave the sins of people who had never seen Him before. He pronounced railing judgments on the most spiritually minded people of His day and warned that on the Day of Judgment, all people would appear before His throne. He claimed that, as the Son, only He could make the Father known. The mystical Jesus, ironically, is a myth.

WHAT'S LEFT?

We have now run out of alternative explanations for Jesus' extraordinary claims. The explanation that He was the world's biggest liar or a lunatic has no takers. The theory that these divine claims were attributed to Jesus in later legends is undermined by the thorough Jewishness of the Gospels and by the fact that the earliest material in the New Testament attests to the same view of Jesus as divine. The notion that Jesus did claim to be divine but in a mystical sense also does not fit the Jewish context of Jesus' teachings and the specific claims that He made.

This leaves only one explanation standing: Jesus did claim to be divine, and He meant it literally (see below).[6]

Ultimately, one of these explanations will have to be chosen; and the only one that fits the evidence is that Jesus truly is Lord.

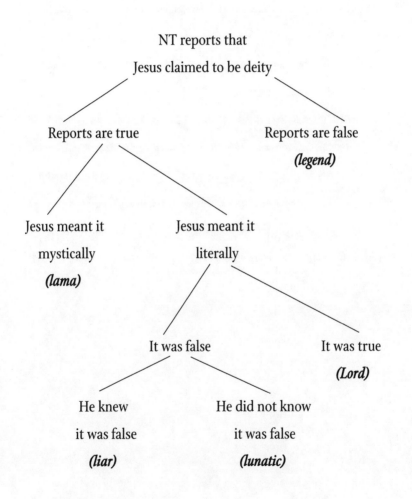

FOR FURTHER READING

Boyd, Gregory A. *Cynic Sage or Son of God? Recovering the Real Jesus in an Age of Revisionist Replies*. Wheaton, Ill.: Victor Books—A BridgePoint Book, 1995. The biblical scholars offering the most sophisticated defenses today of the theory that Jesus was merely a great religious teacher are John Dominic Crossan and Burton L. Mack. Boyd examines their positions and arguments in detail and shows their deep flaws. Boyd gives a shorter, more popular treatment of the same issues in *Jesus Under Siege* (Wheaton, Ill.: Victor Books, 1995).

Kreeft, Peter. *Between Heaven and Hell: A Dialog Somewhere Beyond Death with John F. Kennedy, C. S. Lewis and Aldous Huxley*. Downers Grove, Ill.: InterVarsity Press, 1982. Kennedy, Lewis, and Huxley all happened to die on the same day. Kreeft imagines a dialog between the three men as they await their final disposition, with Lewis defending Christianity in answer to the challenges of Kennedy the humanist and Huxley the mystic. The centerpiece of Lewis's case is the evidence of Jesus' claims to deity.

15

THE EVIDENCE OF JESUS' DEATH

> THE DEATH OF JESUS HOLDS THE
> KEY TO HIS IDENTITY AND TO THE
> NATURE AND LOVE OF GOD.

The central claim of Christianity is that God has acted to restore us

to a sound relationship with Him through Jesus Christ. The crucial way

in which Jesus does this, according to the New Testament, is by His

death on the cross. As bizarre as it may seem, Jesus' main claim to fame,

as it were, was not His teachings or healings but His death. The Gospels

report Jesus as stating that His very purpose in life was to die for others.

"The Son of Man did not come to be served, but to serve, and to give His

life a ransom for many" (Mark 10:45 NKJV). The most famous verse of the

Bible puts it like this: "For God so loved the world, that he gave his only begotten Son, that whosoever believeth in him should not perish, but have everlasting life" (John 3:16 KJV).

The critical question here is whether Christianity has any basis for viewing the death of a Jewish carpenter two thousand years ago as revealing God's love for human beings. But before we can consider the evidence for the significance of Jesus' death, we must first be sure that Jesus died. Surprisingly, many people think He didn't die at all—and quite a few more have speculated that He didn't die when the Bible says He did.

> *God demonstrates His own love toward us, in that while we were still sinners, Christ died for us.*
> —PAUL (ROMANS 5:8 NKJV)

HE'S DEAD, JIM!

That Jesus really died is widely regarded as the most definitively established fact about Jesus that we know. For example, John Dominic Crossan, a former Roman Catholic priest who denies the resurrection of Jesus, agrees that "Jesus' death by execution under Pontius Pilate is as sure as anything historical can ever be."[1] All four Gospels report Jesus' crucifixion and state clearly that He died. The rest of the New Testament is in full agreement that Jesus died on a Roman cross. Furthermore, extrabiblical historical sources—such as the Roman historian Tacitus, the Jewish historian Josephus, and the Talmud—all confirm as fact that Jesus was crucified.[2] No first-century document so much as mentions as a rumor the idea that Jesus did not die on the cross. Moreover, given the revulsion with which everyone in the ancient world viewed crucifixion,[3] at least some of Jesus' followers would have jumped at the chance to claim that the reports of His death by crucifixion were a mistake.

Nevertheless, the death of Jesus on the cross is also frequently denied today. Two theories that deny Jesus died that day require our attention.

THEY GOT THE WRONG GUY?

By far the most widely held theory denying Jesus' death on the cross is the doctrine of Islam, which states that Jesus never died. According to the Qur'an, Islam's scripture, the Jews claimed to have slain Jesus son of Mary, but "they slew him not nor crucified him, but it appeared so unto them," rather, "Allah took him up unto Himself" (Sura 4:157-158). In other words, Jesus only appeared to have been crucified; instead, Jesus was exalted or ascended directly to Heaven without ever dying. According to Muslim tradition, someone else—Judas Iscariot is the most often suggested—got mistakenly crucified by the Romans. About a billion people in the world are taught this view as part of the religion of Islam.

Serious difficulties face anyone seeking to defend the Muslim position on historical grounds because there is no historical evidence for it.[4] The Jewish leaders had seen Jesus in the Temple and around Jerusalem for several days prior to His death, and they would certainly have known (and objected) if the Romans were crucifying the wrong man. We have at least two independent accounts informing us that various friends and family members of Jesus (including His mother) witnessed His death and burial (Luke 23:49-56; John 19:25-27, 38-42).

To get around this evidence, Muslims sometimes claim that God miraculously made Judas (or whoever the crucified man was) look exactly like Jesus. Some even say that it was not a real man at all but only something God made to appear that *looked* like Jesus (sort of a virtual or holographic Jesus). At least three objections may be brought against these explanations. First, there is no evidence for them; the explanations are sheer speculation. Second, the explanations are *ad hoc*. That's a fancy Latin expression used in the science of logic for an answer that has nothing in its favor except that it extricates one's position from a difficulty. (As we will see in the next couple of chapters, *ad hoc* theories are a dime a dozen when it comes to explaining the evidence pertaining to the resurrection of Jesus.) In this instance, the only reason for the suggestion that God miraculously made the crucified man (or whatever it was!) look like Jesus is to save the theory (for which, again, there is absolutely no evidence) that it wasn't Jesus on the cross. Third, the theory implicates God in a deception—one that resulted, according to Islam, in the religion of Christianity being founded on the mistaken idea that Jesus had died on the cross.

THEY DIDN'T FINISH THE JOB?

The other theory denying that Jesus died on the cross admits that He was crucified but claims that Jesus merely passed out, or became unconscious, on the cross. Whereas the Muslim view acknowledges the reality of miracles and is motivated by a pious dislike of the notion that Jesus died, this "swoon" theory is based on skepticism concerning all miracles and is motivated by a naturalistic dislike of the notion that Jesus rose from the dead. This hasn't stopped some Muslim apologists from using the swoon theory, though, as a kind of backup explanation.

The details of this theory as to what exactly happened vary from skeptic to skeptic. Jesus may be admitted to have been very near death—perhaps even "clinically dead." Somehow He revived, perhaps as a result of His body lying in the cool air of the tomb. Perhaps the heavy spices and fragrances with which His body had been hastily anointed for burial contributed in some way. (Talk about aromatherapy!) In some versions Jesus survived the crucifixion only for a very short time, as in Hugh Schonfield's book *The Passover Plot.*[5] In other versions, Jesus lived for many years after His crucifixion. For example, according to the book *Holy Blood, Holy Grail,* after His crucifixion Jesus married Mary Magdalene, moved to the south of France, and had children![6] Barbara Thiering, in her book *Jesus the Man,* also thinks that Jesus ran off with Mary Magdalene after surviving His crucifixion. She claims that Judas Iscariot and Simon Magus (the magician mentioned in Acts 8:9-24) were the other two men crucified alongside Jesus, that all three men survived the ordeal, and that Simon Magus administered medical treatment to Jesus in a cave where their bodies had been left for dead.[7] The essential point, according to all versions of this theory, is that His revival was a purely natural occurrence, the resuscitation of a body that had been barely hanging on to life, not the resurrection of a body that had died.

At least two sets of problems attach themselves to all varieties of the swoon theory. The first is that the theory requires us to pick and choose only those elements of the Gospel accounts of Jesus' crucifixion and burial that seem to help the theory and reject or modify those elements that don't. For example, all versions of the swoon theory make much of the fact that Pilate was surprised that Jesus was dead after being on the cross only for about six hours (Mark 15:25, 33-34, 44). However, the fact that a centurion verified Jesus' death must be discounted or explained away (verse 45), as must the fact that the tomb was sealed with a stone (verse 46). Swoon theorists sometimes suggest that the earthquake reported in Matthew 28:2 was responsible for the stone being moved away from the entrance to the tomb, allowing Jesus to make good His escape. Other skeptics, though, who admit that Jesus died, typically view the earthquake as a legendary embellishment. Advocates of the swoon theory must also dismiss or explain away John's report that a soldier pierced Jesus' side with a spear, despite

John's insistence that he was an eyewitness to the event and that he was telling the truth (John 19:34-35).

The other problem facing all swoon theories is that they don't really account for the *belief* that Jesus had risen from the dead. Keep in mind that the Church did not think of Jesus as a kind of holy Houdini, narrowly escaping the jaws of death. They believed that He had risen from the dead with immortal, exalted life. Jesus had been beaten and crucified. Even if somehow He had survived the ordeal, He would have been too weak and bloodied to have convinced anyone that He was the immortal, glorified Messiah (assuming He would have been so dishonest as to make that claim).

> IT IS IMPOSSIBLE THAT A BEING WHO HAD STOLEN HALF-DEAD OUT OF THE SEPULCHER, WHO CREPT ABOUT WEAK AND ILL, WANTING MEDICAL TREATMENT, WHO REQUIRED BANDAGING, STRENGTHENING AND INDULGENCE, AND WHO STILL AT LAST YIELDED TO HIS SUFFERINGS, COULD HAVE GIVEN TO HIS DISCIPLES THE IMPRESSION THAT HE WAS A CONQUEROR OVER DEATH AND THE GRAVE, THE PRINCE OF LIFE.
>
> —DAVID STRAUSS (A NINETEENTH-CENTURY SKEPTIC)[8]

THE EVIDENCE OF JESUS' DEATH

What's Wrong with This Picture?

We find it interesting and instructive that some skeptics, driven to deny the miracle of the resurrection, feel compelled to deny that Jesus even died at all. After all, people die every day. The Romans crucified many thousands of people (and so were quite proficient at it, by the way). Why are so many people skeptical of the seemingly mundane claim that Jesus died?

The simple answer is that Jesus' death cannot be safely related to a broader view of Jesus and the world if the Christian explanation of its meaning is denied. According to the New Testament, Jesus died in order to atone for our sins, or, to put it another way, to reconcile us to God. To admit this answer, though, would mean recognizing Jesus as the only Savior, the only One who can restore us to a relationship with God. Not surprisingly, religions other than Christianity uniformly reject this claim. But if Jesus did not die for our sins, then why did He die? Here the skeptics and the non-Christian religions join hands in saying either that Jesus did not die after all (or at least not by crucifixion) or that, if He did die, His death had no special significance; Jesus' death, assuming for the sake of argument that it happened, was a tragedy or a miscarriage of justice, but that is all.

One problem with this assessment of Jesus' death is that there is good evidence to show that His death did have cosmic, redemptive significance. First of all, there is solid evidence that Jesus himself expected His death to have this significance. All four Gospels report Jesus predicting His suffering and death in a wide variety of settings and types of sayings. For example, the parable of the wicked vine-growers who kill the owner's son (Matthew 21:33-46; Mark 12:1-12; Luke 20:9-19) clearly refers to Jesus' impending death. The anointing of Jesus' body for burial by Mary of Bethany is presented emphatically as an event that would be remembered wherever the Gospel was preached (Matthew 26:6-13; Mark 14:3-9; John 12:3-8). The institution of the Lord's Supper, which commemorates Jesus' death as a sacrificial act, is found not only in three of the Gospels (Matthew 26:26-29; Mark 14:22-25; Luke 22:15-20) but also in letters written by Paul, who speaks of it as a tradition that he had passed on to the Corinthians (1 Corinthians 11:23-25). Surely the possibility must be at least entertained that Jesus did in fact know that He was going to die, and He knew why.

Another problem with denying the redemptive significance of Jesus' death is that such a cosmic meaning is clearly validated by His subsequent resurrection from the dead. Indeed, the real reason why many skeptics deny the death of Jesus is because it is a simple way to deny the resurrection of Jesus. The presupposition of the resurrection of Jesus—the historical fact that must first of all be true for the resurrection even to make sense—is that Jesus had died. You can't get up if you haven't fallen down, and you can't rise from the dead if you haven't first died. So many skeptics and others committed to denying the resurrection of Jesus argue that He didn't rise because He didn't die—or at least not when He is reported to have died.

That Jesus rose from the dead is of course an astonishing claim, and we don't begrudge the skeptic's request for evidence. Surely, though, the burden of proof rests on anyone who would deny that Jesus died on the cross. The evidence clearly poses a problem in this regard. Moreover, there is additional evidence that Jesus rose from the dead. We will consider that evidence in the next two chapters.

FOR FURTHER READING

Geisler, Norman L. *Encyclopedia of Christian Apologetics.* Grand Rapids: Baker, 1999. The articles on "Christ's Death" (142-50) give a good overview and response to Muslim arguments against Jesus' having died.

Hengel, Martin. *Crucifixion in the Ancient World and the Folly of the Message of the Cross.* Philadelphia: Fortress Press, 1977. Excellent historical study on the significance of crucifixion in New Testament times and later.

16
THE EVIDENCE OF JESUS' EMPTY TOMB

> THE EMPTY TOMB OF JESUS IS A
> COLD, HARD FACT THAT EVEN EARLY
> CRITICS COULDN'T DENY.

If Jesus had merely *claimed* to be the divine Son of God and the
Savior of the world, one might be excused for dismissing or doubting
His claim. But the startling testimony of His followers—and of at least
one former enemy of His followers, the apostle Paul—is that Jesus rose
bodily from the grave. If that's true, Jesus' claims have just about the
strongest corroboration one could want. Imagine you meet a guy who
claims to be God's Son and to have come from Heaven so that everybody
can know His Father like He does. Naturally, you're going to want some
proof. Suppose He tells you that He'll prove it by dying and then rising

from the dead three days later. And then He pulls it off! Wouldn't that convince you?

OK, you say, that would be pretty convincing. But we weren't there. How can we know that Jesus rose from the dead? Couldn't there be another explanation? In this chapter and the next, we present two lines of evidence that together make a compelling case for the resurrection of Jesus as a historical fact. Consider this evidence and see what you think.

I delivered to you as of first importance what I also received, that Christ died for our sins according to the Scriptures, and that he was buried, and that he was raised on the third day according to the Scriptures.
—PAUL (1 CORINTHIANS 15:3-4 NASB)

THE CASE FOR THE EMPTY TOMB

According to the Gospels, Jesus was buried in the tomb of Joseph of Arimathea, a member of the Jewish high council known as the Sanhedrin. The burial was done quickly so as to be finished before the Sabbath. The tomb was sealed with a large stone. From archaeological finds, we know that this would have been a disk-shaped stone that probably took a couple of strong men to move. Then, early on the first day of the week, Mary Magdalene and some other women went to the tomb to apply more spices and fragrances to the body. They found the tomb empty and encountered an angel there, who told them that Jesus had risen. The women told Jesus' male disciples, who also went to the tomb to verify that it was empty (Luke 24:12, 24; John 20:3-8). Later, Jesus appeared in bodily form to His disciples, talking and eating with them on various occasions over a period of forty days.

Such is the record of the four Gospels. The question is whether it is true. Two key lines of evidence give strong support to the conclusion that Jesus rose from the dead. The first line of evidence shows that Jesus was buried in a tomb and that the tomb was later found empty. For the rest of this chapter, we will be focusing on this line of evidence. The second line of evidence shows that numerous individuals saw Jesus alive after His tomb was found empty. We will develop that line of evidence in the next chapter.

Several facts, when considered together, make a formidable case for the empty tomb.

JESUS WAS BURIED

That Jesus was given a formal burial may be regarded as virtually certain. First of all, Paul's statement that Christ "was buried" is part of a stylized confession about Christ that Paul had received as part of the apostolic teaching and had passed on to the Corinthians (see our quotation of 1 Corinthians 15:3-4 at the beginning of this chapter). If we correlate this fact with Paul's visits to see Peter and the other apostles, we find that he must have picked up this confessional statement from them no more than three years or so after Jesus' death (Galatians 1:18-21; 2:1; compare Acts 9:30; 15:2). Even Gerd Lüdemann, a skeptical New Testament scholar who has written extensively against belief in Jesus' resurrection, agrees; he dates this pre-Pauline confession to within two years of Jesus' death.[1] Of course, all four Gospels agree that Jesus was buried.

The evidence from Paul and the Gospels convinces nearly all biblical scholars that Jesus was in fact buried. A notorious exception is John Dominic Crossan, who theorizes that the Roman soldiers threw Jesus' body into a ditch where it was eaten by dogs.[2] Since only the Romans knew what had happened to the body, Crossan says, "those who cared did not know where it was, and those who knew did not care."[3] If

Crossan were correct, the first Christians would have had no reason to think that Jesus had ever been buried. Nor, according to Crossan, would that have mattered to them, since he thinks that they experienced visions of Jesus that convinced them, not that he was physically alive but that his spiritual presence was still with them. Yet those same Christians, within the space of a few short years, formulated a confession that included the affirmation that Jesus had been buried before being raised. Crossan's theory, then, simply does not fit the facts.

JESUS WAS BURIED IN A TOMB

According to all four Gospels, Jesus was not buried in an open cemetery or field but in a rock tomb. They report that a member of the Jewish Sanhedrin named Joseph of Arimathea got permission from Pilate to take Jesus' body down from the cross. He then laid the linen-wrapped body in the tomb and rolled a stone in front of the entrance to the tomb. Matthew, Mark, and Luke all report that women who knew Jesus watched while His body was buried.

There are very good reasons to view the burial of Jesus' body in a tomb as historical fact. First of all, it is attested in all four Gospels, and there is no alternative account anywhere from the first century.

Second, the differences in wording among the four accounts make it likely that we have two or three independent versions of the burial story. For example, whereas Mark writes, "Joseph of Arimathea . . . went in before Pilate, and asked for the body of Jesus" (Mark 15:43 NASB), both Matthew and Luke write, "This man went to Pilate and asked for the body of Jesus" (Matthew 27:58; Luke 23:52 NASB). The precise verbal agreement between Matthew and Luke here proves that either one of them used the other or, more likely, both used a common source.[4] The differences between John and the other three Gospels are more marked and clearly show John's independence from them on this matter.[5]

Third, there are good reasons to think that the account of Jesus' burial dated from considerably before Mark was written. The existence of other parallel accounts independent of Mark makes this likely. Furthermore, the burial narrative appears to be part of a continuous "passion narrative," or account of Jesus' last supper, arrest, trials, and execution, which most Gospel scholars think existed before Mark. The four Gospel versions of this passion narrative show more continuity and exhibit greater parallels to one another than the rest of the Gospel material. Indeed, the passion narrative is probably the oldest Gospel material to receive definite form, as Paul's quotation from the last-supper section of that narrative confirms (1 Corinthians 11:23-25). A judicious assessment of the evidence would seem to call for dating the passion narrative, including the burial account, to the early 40s at the latest or no more than about ten years after Jesus' death (and of course it might be even older than that).

Fourth, the burial accounts are all brief, simple, and free of any apparent theologizing or miraculous elements to which skeptics might object. Of course, we believe that an account should not be rejected merely because it has theological or miraculous elements. Our point here is that the lack of any such elements places the burden of proof on those who would question their reliability.

Fifth, Mark's account, which is generally regarded as the earliest, is not written in an apologetic or defensive manner. In other words, Mark's account of the burial does not seem to be written with the intent of defending the claim that Jesus rose from the dead. For one thing, Mark reports Pilate's surprise that Jesus had already died, a bit of information that he could have suppressed but didn't. Mark does mention that the centurion verified the death (Mark 15:44-45), but he does not emphasize the point or give any elaboration.

Now, admittedly the other Gospels contain additional pieces of information that could legitimately be described as apologetic in significance. We can understand some skepticism about some of those later pieces of information (though we don't share that skepticism). But even if we strip away all of those bits, the earliest, core account remains intact and unimpeachable. Skeptical scholars sometimes try to discredit the empty tomb on the grounds that the later Gospels supposedly embellish the story of Jesus' burial. Such a criticism is illogical, since later embellishments by other authors cannot undermine the credibility of the original account.

IN COMPARISON WITH THE APOCRYPHAL STORIES OF LATER CENTURIES, THE TOMB STORIES [IN THE GOSPELS] SHOW LITTLE ELABORATION OF MIRACULOUS DETAIL. IN COMPARISON WITH DEVELOPMENTS IN NEW TESTAMENT MATERIALS, THEY DO NOT SHOW EXTENSIVE INFLUENCES FROM OLD TESTAMENT PASSAGES. HENCE, WE MUST PRESUME THAT THE STORY IS EARLY AND THAT THERE WAS NO CLEAR EVIDENCE TO CONTROVERT IT.

—PHEME PERKINS[6]

Sixth, it is unlikely that Joseph of Arimathea's involvement was fictitious. Given the fact that all four Gospels assign some measure of responsibility to the Sanhedrin for Jesus' execution, it would be surprising, to put it mildly, for someone to invent the story of a Sanhedrin member taking care of Jesus' burial. One would have expected pious fiction to have assigned this loving duty to one of the apostles, or to one of Jesus' other friends, such as Simon the (former) leper (Mark 14:3) or the family of Mary, Martha, and Lazarus of Bethany or a relative of John the Baptist—*anyone* but a member of the Sanhedrin! If we are right in dating the passion and burial narrative to the 40s or earlier, it would also seem highly unlikely that anyone would make up a story about a member of the Sanhedrin burying Jesus' body, since too many people would have been in a position to dispute such a fiction.

The most common objection to the Gospel reports that Jesus was buried in a tomb is that Paul does not mention a tomb anywhere in his epistles. This objection is an argument from silence and so by itself is rather weak. The Book of Acts does report Paul mentioning the tomb in one of his evangelistic speeches: "When they [the Jewish rulers] had fulfilled all that was written of him, they took him down from the tree, and laid him in a tomb" (Acts 13:29). Of course, Luke knows that one member of the Sanhedrin in particular, Joseph of Arimathea, was responsible for burying Jesus, and he distances that member from the rest of the Sanhedrin (Luke 23:50-51). The fact that Luke knows this detail but reports Paul as speaking more generally about the Sanhedrin condemning Jesus and burying Him is best explained by concluding that Luke is reporting accurately what Paul actually said.

For all of the above reasons, we may confidently state that Jesus was buried in a tomb by Joseph of Arimathea.

THE TOMB IS EMPTY

Having established that Jesus was buried in a tomb, it becomes difficult to deny the Gospel reports that the tomb was found empty a few days after the burial. Again, multiple evidences support this conclusion.

First, as with the burial story, all four Gospels report that the tomb was found empty.

Second, the Gospels present at least two independent accounts of the discovery of the empty tomb, since John's account is markedly different from those of the other three Gospels. Indeed, critics often argue that the accounts cannot be accepted because they seem to be almost impossible to reconcile with each other in certain details. But the apparent contradictions in the accounts actually prove that the accounts are independent of one another. Just as discrepancies in the accounts of a traffic accident given by different eyewitnesses cannot disprove that the accident occurred but rather prove that their accounts were not rehearsed together, so also the difficulties of harmonizing the Gospel accounts of the discovery of the empty tomb confirm the core fact to which all of those accounts testify.

Third, as with Mark's burial account, his account of the discovery of the empty tomb is free of apologetic material and virtually free of miraculous or theological elements. The "young man" in a white robe who tells the women that Jesus has risen (Mark 16:5) is presumably an angel, as Matthew makes explicit (Matthew 28:5). But Mark's description lacks any overtly supernatural elements and is told in a very matter-of-fact manner. Again, the later Gospel accounts do include additional material, some of which may fairly be considered theological or apologetic in significance (which is not to prejudge their factual nature). But the core narrative as seen in Mark has no such elements to which a skeptic might plausibly appeal as the basis for deeming the story to be a pious fiction.

Fourth, Matthew's account of the guard at the tomb (Matthew 28:11-15), even if viewed with some skepticism as an apologetic fiction, confirms that the tomb was empty. You see, Matthew's account reflects a dispute in the first century between Jews and Christians in which *both sides* agreed not only that the tomb was empty but that it had been guarded. (By a "guard" is meant, not a single individual but a guard unit consisting of several soldiers, as Matthew makes explicit in 28:4, 11.) As William Lane Craig explains,[7] the dispute went something like this:

Christian: "The Lord is risen!"

Jew: "No, his disciples stole away his body."

Christian: "The guard at the tomb would have prevented any such theft."

Jew: "No, the guard fell asleep."

Christian: "The chief priests bribed the guard to say this."

Let's be skeptical for the sake of argument and assume that the claim that the chief priests bribed the guard to say they fell asleep is a Christian apologetic fiction. The only reason to make up such a claim would be to counter the Jewish claim that the guard actually had fallen asleep. (Surely Matthew would not have invented *that* claim.) In turn, the Jewish opponents of Christianity would never have suggested that the guard fell asleep (true or not) unless they conceded that the tomb had been guarded. Thus, even if we assume that Matthew is making up the bit about the guard being bribed, it makes no sense to charge him with making up the whole story. Clearly both Christians and Jews in Matthew's community agreed that Jesus' body was buried in a tomb, the tomb was guarded, and the tomb was found empty. Indeed, the Jewish claim that Jesus' disciples stole His body is the earliest non-Christian alternative explanation for the empty tomb on record. It's hard to find anyone today who will seriously contend that this explanation is correct. In any case, the explanation concedes as fact that Jesus' body was buried in a tomb and that the tomb became empty.

Fifth, there is archaeological evidence that shows it is very likely that the Jewish polemical claim that the disciples had stolen the body dated from very soon after the Christian movement began. In Paris there is a white marble slab from Nazareth that has a decree of Caesar written on it that dates about A.D. 45-50. The decree orders that tombs "shall remain undisturbed in perpetuity" and decrees that anyone removing bodies from such tombs will be subject to capital punishment. Evidently Claudius, who was Caesar from A.D. 41 to 54, associated tomb-robbery with the unrest in Rome between Jews and Christians during his reign.

In A.D. 49 he expelled all Jews from Rome because of that unrest, which the Roman writer Suetonius in his biography of Claudius blamed on "Chrestus," that is, Christ. The decree threatening capital punishment for disturbing tombs, then, may have been prompted by the hearsay that Jesus' disciples had stolen the body. If this is correct, as seems likely, the rumor about the disciples stealing the body dates from at least the 40s, when most of the Jewish leaders who presided over Jesus' condemnation were still alive. This is another piece of early evidence, then, that the tomb was empty.

Sixth, the Gospels agree that the first persons to discover the empty tomb were women followers of Jesus, not His male apostles. Specifically, all four Gospels identify Mary Magdalene as the leading woman who made this discovery when she went to the tomb early Sunday morning. It is improbable in the extreme that male writers would invent such a story. The point here is not merely that the Gospels might have been expected to give this honor to Peter or John or one of the other apostles. One might plausibly explain away this surprising feature as consistent with the Gospels' emphasis on the slowness of Jesus' apostles to believe. But still, Mark or his source, if the empty tomb was fiction, was unlikely to have made women be the first to discover the empty tomb. Again, Jesus' male friends Simon and

Lazarus in Bethany or better yet Joseph of Arimathea would have been suitable candidates, if the story was pure fiction.

Why would women not have been assigned this honor in a pious fiction? For the simple reason that a woman's testimony was considered of little or no value. As Pinchas Lapide observes, "In a purely fictional narrative one would have avoided making women the crown witnesses of the resurrection since they were considered in rabbinic Judaism as incapable of giving valid testimony."[8] Lapide, it should be noted, is a Jewish scholar who admits that Jesus rose from the dead but who declines to accept the idea of Jesus as the Messiah.

THE CASE OF THE MISSING BODY

OK, we've seen that Jesus' body was buried in a tomb and that a few days later the tomb was found to be empty. Jesus' body was not there. The Gospels' own explanation is well known: God raised Jesus from the dead. Some skeptics, though, while acknowledging the empty tomb, have tried to explain it in some other way.

We have already mentioned the earliest explanation, which came from some Jewish opponents of Christianity—that the disciples stole the body. For sake of argument, we'll forget about the guard (though those same opponents admitted the guard was there). Even if the disciples had had the opportunity to steal the body, they didn't have a motive for doing so. The execution of Jesus on a cross would have marked Him in their eyes as a false prophet or false Messiah. Why would they steal the body? No convincing answer to this question has ever been given.

Another explanation that has sometimes been advanced is that the women went to the wrong tomb. Honestly, this explanation smacks of desperation. The Gospels report that the women watched Jesus being buried (e.g., Mark 15:47), so they knew where the correct tomb was. And even if they didn't, historically it has been men, not women, who have been reluctant to ask for directions! More seriously, it is absurd to think that the women would have gone to the wrong tomb and immediately jumped to the conclusion that Jesus had risen. It is even more absurd to claim that none of the women or the men would have discovered this mistake.

The best explanation for the empty tomb will be based not only on the fact of the empty tomb in isolation but will also take into consideration what happened after the tomb was found empty: Jesus appeared to both women and men followers over a period of time. We will consider the evidence of those appearances in the next chapter.

FOR FURTHER READING

Craig, William Lane. *Knowing the Truth about the Resurrection: Our Response to the Empty Tomb.* Ann Arbor, Mich.: Servant Books, 1991. Craig may be the most published author in history on the resurrection of Jesus; this is an excellent overview of the subject written for a general readership.

Walker, Peter. *The Weekend that Changed the World: The Mystery of Jerusalem's Empty Tomb.* Louisville, Ky.: Westminster John Knox Press, 2000. Interesting exposition of the events surrounding the discovery of the empty tomb, offering numerous specific details based on archaeological research.

17

THE EVIDENCE OF JESUS' RESURRECTION APPEARANCES

THE ACCOUNTS OF JESUS' APPEAR-
ANCES CANNOT BE REASONABLY
EXPLAINED AWAY.

An empty tomb by itself would be merely a mystery. However, the
Gospels report that the day it was found empty, people started seeing
Jesus alive. Again, such appearances by themselves might be dismissed
as subjective visions or even hallucinations (though only with extreme
difficulty, as we shall explain). But the twin facts of the empty tomb and
the experiences of Jesus' followers seeing Him alive after the tomb was
found empty, *when taken together,* become compelling evidences for the
conclusion that Jesus was indeed alive. But if, as we saw in chapter 15,

Jesus had indeed died on the cross, then the only logical conclusion is that Jesus rose from the dead.

To these He also presented Himself alive after His suffering, by many convincing proofs, appearing to them over a period of forty days and speaking of the things concerning the kingdom of God.

—LUKE (ACTS 1:3 NASB)

JESUS' APPEARANCES TO WOMEN

The Gospels report that women friends were not only the first people to find the tomb to be empty, but they were also the first to see Him alive. As we explained in the previous chapter with respect to the empty tomb, male disciples would surely not have made up a story about Jesus rising from the dead and make women the first witnesses. If not Peter or John, a myth-making man would have had the first witnesses to Jesus' resurrection be some other men, such as Lazarus of Bethany or Joseph of Arimathea.

Actually, in the interests of full disclosure, we should point out that the first witness to the risen Jesus would have been viewed as unreliable for reasons that went beyond her being female. Mary Magdalene, whom all four Gospels name as the first person to see Jesus alive, had been delivered by Jesus from seven demons during His Galilean ministry (Luke 8:2). We can just hear it now—indeed, if this had happened even in our day, we would be hearing: "You say He's risen from the dead? And who saw Him first? Some hysterical females—including that crazy Mary!"

Please understand us: We don't think Mary was crazy, and we wouldn't condone dismissing the testimony of women as borne of hysteria. But such a dim view was taken of women's testimony generally in the first century that men simply would not have taken them seriously. In such a climate, it would have been unthinkable for one or more Christian men to have made up the story of women being the first to see Jesus alive from the dead:

"OK, Barney, the tomb's empty. Now, who shall we say Jesus appears to first?"

"Uh, I dunno, Mark . . . how about one of the women?"

"Sure! All right—which one should we mention first?"

"Well. . . . hey, how about Mary Magdalene?"

"You mean that nutty dame that had all those demons in her? Great idea, Barn!"

"Ah-heh-heh-heh! OK, Mark, write it down!"

The conclusion seems almost unavoidable: The Gospels report women as having been the first to see Jesus alive from the dead because in fact they were the first people to have such an experience. Small wonder, then, that almost all biblical scholars today, even those who are highly skeptical of the resurrection, agree that the women did have such an experience and at least *thought* that they saw Jesus.

JESUS' APPEARANCES TO HIS MALE DISCIPLES

The story of Jesus' resurrection would have gotten no traction if the resurrection appearances had been limited to a small group of women. According to both the Gospels and Paul's epistles, Jesus also appeared to

His male disciples, both individually and in groups, over a period of time following the first report of His resurrection.

Let's go back to Paul's treatment of the resurrection in 1 Corinthians 15. As we mentioned in the previous chapter, the traditional or confessional material that Paul rehearsed at the beginning of 1 Corinthians 15 apparently was derived from the Jerusalem apostles and was handed on to Paul during his first visit with them just a few years after Jesus' death. New Testament scholars disagree among themselves as to whether the confession or "creed" itself that begins in verse 3 runs only to verse 5 or continues to verse 7. For our purposes, though, it doesn't much matter, since we can be sure that Paul derived the list of witnesses in verses 5-7 from that same visit. How do we know this? Well, the two appearances of Jesus to single individuals that Paul mentions in the passage (other than Jesus' appearance to Paul himself) were to "Cephas" (verse 5) and "James" (verse 7). (Cephas [pronounced KEY-fuss] was the Aramaic name for "Peter," and, like the Greek *Petros,* means "Rock.") Now, those happen to be the two apostles whom Paul met in his first visit to Jerusalem after his conversion (Galatians 1:18-19).

We may conclude, then, that Paul's list of resurrection appearances was derived directly from Peter and James and dated from just a few years after those appearances would have taken place. That makes his list about as reliable as one could reasonably ask.

What about the Gospel accounts of Jesus' appearances to His male disciples? First of all, the unimpeachable character of the same Gospels' accounts of Jesus' appearances to women followers lends considerable credibility to their accounts of His appearances to the men. At some point, we ought to recognize that the Gospel writers were trying in good faith to tell what really happened, since so much of what they say has clear marks of candor even with regard to facts embarrassing to their cause.

Second, the discordant nature of the Gospel accounts of Jesus' resurrection appearances suggests their independence and therefore the reliability of those facts on which they agree. In our opinion, most of the alleged contradictions among the accounts can be resolved, though some only with difficulty.[1] But this difficulty is consistent with the context of the events: Jesus' disciples would still have been feeling shock and grief, and the appearances occurred without warning and were totally surprising. As Ian Wilson, who accepts the existence of intractable contradictions in the accounts, observes, "In their own way the garblings and inconsistencies have the same quality as the memories of witnesses after a road accident, which are, after all, personal and often highly confused versions of the same story."[2]

Third, Paul's list in 1 Corinthians 15 provides independent confirmation of the appearances recounted in narrative detail by the writers of the Gospels and Acts. His wording is quite different from theirs and includes one major appearance that is not reported or implied in any Gospel, showing that neither can be regarded as based on the other (see the table below).[3]

1 Corinthians 15	Gospels
"Cephas," i.e., Peter (v. 5)	Simon, i.e., Simon Peter (Luke 24:34)
"The twelve," i.e., the body of twelve apostles, which at the time was missing one (v. 5)	The "eleven" disciples (Luke 24:33, 36-49; John 20:19-23)
"More than five hundred brethren at one time" (v. 6)	Unknown
"James" (v. 7), i.e., James the brother of Jesus (cf. Galatians 1:19)	A resurrection appearance is implied for James the brother of Jesus by his position as an apostle (Acts 12:17; 15:13; 21:18)
"All the apostles" (v. 7)	Probably refers to the last appearance to all the apostles, as in Acts 1:4-11 (note Acts 1:15)
"And last of all, as to one untimely born, He appeared also to me" (v. 8)	Paul's experience recounted in detail three times (Acts 9:1-19; 22:3-16; 26:12-18)

We do think that Luke was dependent upon Paul for the details of his (Paul's) encounters with the risen Jesus. However, it is clear that Luke did not base the resurrection narrative in his Gospel on Paul's list in 1 Corinthians 15. In other respects the resurrection narratives of the other three Gospels appear completely independent of Paul. From these independent sources, then, we may confidently conclude that Peter was the first of the men to experience an appearance of Jesus and that the body of the Twelve (numbering eleven at the time) also shared such an experience. James the Lord's brother also had this experience as an individual. We also have good evidence of one or more appearances to a wider group of people. Finally, in Paul himself we have an indisputable first-hand testimony of a man who says that he saw the risen Christ.

ADMISSIONS (SOME GRUDGING) OF

THE RESURRECTION APPEARANCES

THAT THE EXPERIENCES DID OCCUR, EVEN IF THEY ARE EXPLAINED IN PURELY NATURAL TERMS, IS A FACT UPON WHICH BOTH BELIEVER AND UNBELIEVER CAN AGREE.

—REGINALD H. FULLER[*]

THEIR TESTIMONIES CANNOT PROVE THEM TO HAVE BEEN RIGHT IN SUPPOSING THAT JESUS HAD RISEN FROM THE DEAD. HOWEVER, THESE ACCOUNTS DO PROVE THAT CERTAIN PEOPLE WERE UTTERLY CONVINCED THAT THAT IS WHAT HE HAD DONE.

—MICHAEL GRANT[5]

THAT JESUS' FOLLOWERS (AND LATER PAUL) HAD RESURRECTION EXPERIENCES IS, IN MY JUDGEMENT, A FACT. WHAT THE REALITY WAS THAT GAVE RISE TO THE EXPERIENCES I DO NOT KNOW.

—E. P. SANDERS[6]

By the way, it's almost impossible to find anyone who will state that Paul was lying about having seen the risen Jesus, for two very good reasons. First, Paul was an arch-opponent of the Christian message, actively persecuting Christians, until his encounter with Christ. Second, for the rest of his life, Paul suffered tremendously, experiencing numerous imprisonments, beatings, and other forms of mistreatment in various cities from non-Christians, as well as opposition from many Christians suspicious of his claims to apostleship. We're not aware of any biblical scholar or historian who claims that Paul was making the whole thing up.

What were these appearances like? Only Luke and John give us any details about what Jesus looked like and how He acted, and skeptics almost uniformly reject these details as later legendary accretions. However, it should be noted that Luke and John give two completely independent accounts of Jesus' resurrection appearances, and they agree in some important details not found in Matthew or Mark:

1. Peter and at least one other apostle ran to the tomb after hearing the women's report and saw the burial wrappings lying by themselves, after which Peter went home (Luke 24:12, 24; John 20:3-10).[7]

2. Jesus' disciples on occasion did not immediately recognize him (Luke 24:16, 31; John 21:4-7).

3. Jesus was able to appear and disappear suddenly, even within a locked room (Luke 24:31, 36; John 20:19, 26).

4. Jesus greeted the disciples with the words, "Peace be with you" (Luke 24:36 KJV; John 20:19, 21, 26).

5. Jesus invited His disciples to inspect His hands and even to touch Him (Luke 24:39-40; John 20:20, 27).

6. Jesus ate fish with His disciples (Luke 24:41-43; John 21:9-15).[8]

Again, the usual response from skeptics is to dismiss the indications that Jesus had a physical body (points 5 and 6 above) as later legendary additions. However, this seems unlikely for a number of reasons.

First, as we have just seen, Luke and John present independent accounts that testify to these same indications of Jesus' materiality.

Second, some skeptics will seize upon the statements indicating that the disciples did not always recognize Jesus immediately and that He was able to appear and disappear suddenly (points 2 and 3 above) as evidence that His body had not been reanimated. Yet these statements (which don't really contradict those statements indicating that Jesus' physical body was alive[9]) also are unique to Luke and John. Thus, at least some skeptics must engage in picking and choosing from the same source material what they will accept as authentic. Ironically, skeptics who reject the mundane, physical characteristics reported of the risen Jesus will sometimes appeal to His reported heavenly, supernatural characteristics!

Third, the notion that Christian belief in Jesus' resurrection developed from a purely spiritual concept to a more materialistic one can be fit into the cultural settings of developing first-century Christianity only with great difficulty, if at all. The Christian movement was exclusively

Jewish for some fifteen years (A.D. 33-48 or so), and its religious and theological leadership (the apostles) remained exclusively Jewish for about
twenty years more (A.D. 49-68 or so). After the fall of Jerusalem in A.D.
70, the composition and leadership of Christianity became increasingly
Gentile, specifically Hellenistic.

Now, the claim that the resurrection was first regarded as a purely
spiritual reality and only around the fall of Jerusalem and afterward
became viewed as the reanimation of Jesus' physical body would work
much better if the cultural shift in early Christianity had been the other
way around. Although Jews entertained various conceptions of the after-
life, the dominant view of resurrection in first-century Jewish thought
was that it entailed the reanimation or reconstruction of the human
body and its endowment with immortality. On the other hand, the
concept of the resurrection of the human body—the flesh—was commonly regarded in Hellenistic culture as absurd; Greeks tended to favor
the view that the person continued existing after death in a shadowy
spiritual state from which there was no return to physical life.[10]

The problem, then, is that skeptical scholars often attribute to the
earliest Christians, all of whom were Jewish, a view of resurrection that
actually corresponds more closely to the Gentile/Greek concept of

spiritual immortality. And they then attribute the belief in a physical resurrection, which was at the time essentially an exclusively Jewish concept, to the growing Gentile presence toward the end of the New Testament period. Something's definitely wrong with this picture!

The Gospel accounts of Jesus' appearances, then, provide independent testimonies to the belief, rooted in the experiences of the earliest, Jewish followers of Jesus, that Jesus had been raised from the dead.

Looking for a Way Out?

If you don't want to believe that Jesus rose physically from the dead to immortal life, you have a cafeteria of alternative explanations for the evidence from which to choose. We've already considered several of these in this and the previous two chapters.

> ONCE YOU ALLOW THAT SOMETHING REMARKABLE HAPPENED TO THE BODY THAT MORNING, ALL THE OTHER DATA FALL INTO PLACE WITH EASE. ONCE YOU INSIST THAT NOTHING SO OUTLANDISH HAPPENED, YOU ARE DRIVEN TO EVER MORE COMPLEX AND FANTASTIC HYPOTHESES.
>
> —N. T. WRIGHT[11]

Some theories admit the empty tomb but deny the appearances. For example, the theory that the women went to the wrong tomb (one that happened to be unoccupied) "explains" the empty tomb but does nothing to account for the appearances. The theory that the disciples stole the body admits the empty tomb but implies that the accounts of Jesus appearing to both women and men are all lies—which as we have seen is essentially impossible.

Other theories admit the appearances but deny the empty tomb. For example, the idea that the Romans crucified the wrong man can explain the appearances (at least to some extent) but leaves the tomb occupied (albeit with the wrong body). The theory that the appearances were hallucinations doesn't explain the appearances all that well (did the disciples have group hallucinations?) and cannot explain the empty tomb at all.

Of the naturalistic theories that attempt to account for both the empty tomb and the appearances, by far the most popular is the view that Jesus was not really dead when His body was laid in the tomb and that somehow He revived (or was revived), left the tomb, and convinced His followers that He had conquered death. As we saw in chapter 15, though, the evidence that Jesus actually died is very strong, and the notion that a barely alive man could have convinced His followers that He had arisen to immortal life is extremely weak.

By far the best explanation for all of the evidence is the consistent claim of the New Testament that God raised Jesus from the dead. The Resurrection not only makes sense of the evidence of the empty tomb and the appearances, it also makes sense of Jesus' claims to be the unique, eternal Son of God. For those who are willing to believe, the resurrection of Jesus may be one of the most compelling evidences that God exists and that He has made himself known in Jesus Christ.

FOR FURTHER READING

Copan, Paul, ed. *Will the Real Jesus Please Stand Up? A Debate between William Lane Craig and John Dominic Crossan.* Moderated by William F. Buckley Jr. With responses from Robert J. Miller, Craig L. Blomberg, Marcus Borg, and Ben Witherington III. Grand Rapids: Baker, 1998. Perhaps the most interesting published debate on the resurrection of Jesus; Craig and Crossan are leading defenders of their respective positions.

Habermas, Gary R. "Resurrection Appearances of Jesus." In *In Defense of Miracles: A Comprehensive Case for God's Action in History,* ed. R. Douglas Geivett and Gary R. Habermas, pp. 262-275. Downers Grove, Ill.: InterVarsity, 1997. Next to Craig, Habermas is probably the most prolific Christian scholar defending the Resurrection.

18

THE EVIDENCE OF THOSE WHO LIVED FOR CHRIST

> ## THE REALITY OF JESUS' RESURRECTION IS EVIDENT IN THOSE WHO HAVE LIVED FOR HIM.

The resurrection of Jesus from the dead should not be viewed as a mere curiosity of the past. It is the confirmation that Jesus' death was not just an unfortunate miscarriage of justice but the means to our reconciliation with God. Jesus' resurrection constitutes a promise to those who believe in Him that they, too, will enjoy eternal, immortal life in a relationship with God.

If this resurrection life that began in Christ and that will become ours is a reality, may we expect there to be some evidence of it in His followers now? Here we must not speculate as to what we ought to find, but rather we should look for what Jesus says we will see as evidence that the message of new life in Him is true. In other words, what did Jesus tell us to look for in the way that His followers live that would be evidence of the reality of His life in them? Two closely related evidences stand out in this regard.

> *If we live, we live to the Lord, and if we die, we die to the Lord; so then, whether we live or whether we die, we are the Lord's. For to this end Christ died and lived again, that he might be Lord both of the dead and of the living.*
> —PAUL (ROMANS 14:8-9)

WHAT TO LOOK FOR IN JESUS' FOLLOWERS

First, Christ's followers would love one another. "By this all people will know that you are my disciples, if you have love for one another" (John 13:35 NASB). The love of Christ would break down barriers of hatred between people.

Second, Christ's followers would proclaim the message of new life in God's eternal kingdom to people of all nations. "Go therefore and make disciples of all nations" (Matthew 28:19). This process of making disciples was not to be one of military conquest but of persuasive proclamation. Thus, making the effort to bring this message to other nations—some unknown, some feared—would require as motivation the love of which Christ spoke.

Is there significant evidence of these signs of Christ's living presence in his people? We confidently say yes, but we need to make note of two crucial qualifications emphasized by Jesus himself.

First, many people who profess to be His followers are not. Toward the end of the Sermon on the Mount, Jesus said, "Not every one who says to me, 'Lord, Lord,' shall enter the kingdom of heaven, but he who does the will of my Father who is in heaven" (Matthew 7:21). In one of His most famous analogies, Jesus said that at the end of history, His good and wicked servants would be separated like sheep from goats, with only the sheep enjoying eternal life (Matthew 25:31-46; compare verses 14-30). Indeed, Jesus predicted that many false prophets would arise in His name (Matthew 7:22-23; 24:11, 24) and that many people who professed to follow Him would prove unfaithful (Matthew 24:11-12). Regrettably, Jesus, was without a doubt, right on the money in this regard. The history of Christianity is littered with people claiming to speak in His name and doing all sorts of evil things, often under the guise of following Christ. While it might be going too far to view this "dark side" of Christianity as evidence supporting faith in Christ, surely it does not make sense to reject Christ because of the actions of those who are unfaithful to Him.

Second, the evidences of Christ's living presence were not expected to be manifested fully in individuals the moment they began to follow Christ, nor were those evidences expected to be fully realized in the Church from the outset. Rather, these evidences were expected to *grow*. Jesus compared the kingdom of God to the mustard seed, which starts off very tiny but becomes a huge tree (Matthew 13:31-32). When Jesus told His original followers to "make disciples of all nations," He made it clear that this would be a long process of education that would have to continue until His return at the end of the age: "teaching them to observe all that I have commanded you; and lo, I am with you always, to the close of the age" (Matthew 28:19-20). Likewise, Jesus predicted that the Church would reach all nations with His message, but that doing so would take until the end (Matthew 24:14). So, while we should expect these evidences of Christ's living presence to be significant, we should also understand that individuals are at different stages in their development as disciples and that the Church as a whole also has been going through a process of maturing in its relationship with Christ.

With these qualifications in mind, is there significant evidence of Christ's resurrection presence in His people?

"SEE HOW THEY LOVE ONE ANOTHER"

About A.D. 197 or 198, the theologian Tertullian reported that non-Christians were saying of Christians, "See how they love one another" (*Apologeticum* 39.7). Ironically, this was a backhanded compliment: Tertullian was responding to the criticism that Christians were too soft, too coddling of one another (on the notion that only the strong should survive). The critics lost that argument, though. When Tertullian wrote those words, the Church was in the midst of an incredible period of growth. During the second and third centuries, Christianity grew a thousandfold, from a small sect of about seven thousand people to about seven *million* adherents—all *before* Constantine issued his Edict of Milan ending the persecution of Christianity. While various factors no doubt came into play in this astonishing growth, the love that Christians showed to one another and to other people clearly played a major role.

> BECAUSE CHRISTIANS WERE EXPECTED
> TO AID THE LESS FORTUNATE,
> MANY OF THEM RECEIVED SUCH AID,
> AND ALL COULD FEEL GREATER SECURITY
> AGAINST BAD TIMES. BECAUSE THEY WERE
> ASKED TO NURSE THE SICK AND DYING,
> MANY OF THEM RECEIVED SUCH NURSING.
> BECAUSE THEY WERE ASKED TO LOVE OTHERS,
> THEY IN TURN WERE LOVED. AND IF
> CHRISTIANS WERE REQUIRED TO OBSERVE
> A FAR MORE RESTRICTIVE MORAL CODE
> THAN THAT OBSERVED BY PAGANS,
> CHRISTIANS—ESPECIALLY WOMEN—
> ENJOYED A FAR MORE SECURE FAMILY LIFE.
>
> —RODNEY STARK, SOCIOLOGIST[1]

In too many times and places in church history since, such trans-forming, infectious love has been sorely lacking. On the one hand, the triumph of Christianity politically in the fourth century brought various evils of pagan culture almost to a complete end, such as infanticide, and brought significant advances in the treatment of women (though they did not go far enough). Charitable hospitals, orphanages, homes for the blind, and other such institutions proliferated as soon as Christianity had won its political rights in the fourth century. On the other hand, there is no doubt that the growth of powerful church institutions in European Christianity during the Middle Ages stifled the spirit of Christian love, although it was not completely extinguished. One can see in the monastic tradition, for all its faults, an effort to cultivate Christian love.

During the past three centuries or so, love has become more and more a hallmark of authentic Christianity throughout the world. Christian love and values led to the abolition of slavery in England, the United States (far later than it should, unfortunately), and in all nations around the globe where Christianity was dominant. Most of the humanitarian movements and institutions of the eighteenth and nineteenth centuries were explicitly Christian in origin and philosophy. Some of those institutions, such as the Red Cross and the Salvation Army, are with us to this day. Christians led efforts to reform prisons, to enact child-labor laws, and to educate and feed the poor.[2] They built hospitals and universities; they ran orphanages and women's shelters.

Christian charity (the old-fashioned word for love) continues to this day. Most acts of love never get noticed or reported and cannot be quantified. Consider, though, just one Christian humanitarian institution, World Vision. It was started by a Christian, Bob Pierce, in the 1950s to help Korean children orphaned in the war. It now provides food, clothing, health care, and education to tens of millions of people in over a hundred countries every year. World Vision has dug more than a thousand wells in Africa to provide millions of people there with badly needed clean water. And oh, yes—they also tell people around the world that their motivation for doing these things is so that they will know that God loves them and has acted in Jesus to bring them eternal life. Of course, there are many, many other institutions doing similar work.

If it sounds as if we are bragging, we're not. Most Christians could do a great deal more than they are doing to show love to one another and to the needy of the world. But the fact remains that the love of Christ has been very much a reality to the hundreds of millions of people who have been helped by Christians impelled to share that love with others.

"IN HIM SHALL THE NATIONS HOPE"

As we mentioned, Jesus commanded His followers to make disciples of people from all the nations and predicted that they would do so before His return at the end of the age (Matthew 24:14; 28:19-20). In our day this prediction appears to be on the cusp of fulfillment. There are significant numbers of Christians in almost every country on the earth.

Some two billion people in the world consider themselves Christians, and while many of these may be Christians in name only (a problem that all large religions inevitably have), many of them are clearly genuine.

It is no doubt that serious mistakes have been made throughout the history of Christian missions. For example, it is not surprising to learn that sometimes missionaries from the West have imported their culture along with the Gospel (though Western culture is not all bad, mind you). Overall, though, the spread of the Gospel to every continent has benefited the peoples of the world immeasurably and has demonstrated the power of the risen Christ to change the lives of individuals, families, even whole societies for the better. Consider just one example.

Dr. Rochunga Pudaite grew up in northeast India as part of the Hmar tribe. When a Welsh missionary named Watkin Roberts brought the message of Christ to the Hmar people in the early twentieth century, Rochunga's father, Chawnga, was one of the first to believe. As Chawnga himself observed, Roberts did not try to impose European customs on the Hmars. In fact, Roberts carried on his missionary work in defiance of the local British government representative. (Christian missionaries from the West, far from always being agents of Western cultural or political imperialism, have all too often done their work under opposition from the Western governmental or corporate powers in the region.) However, as thousands of Hmars came to faith in Christ, their way of life did change. "They stopped quarreling, fighting, drinking, and living in fear of evil spirits." Over five hundred Hmars became missionaries, taking food and Bibles to tribes throughout the region, including tribes of former enemies whose heads the Hmar had previously displayed as trophies over the doors of their bamboo huts. They were, as Pudaite puts it, "transformed from headhunters to hearthunters."[3] Pudaite is now president of Bibles For the World, which has sent over fourteen million Bibles to individual homes throughout the world.

> THE RESURRECTION IS A DIVINE BOMBSHELL DROPPED INTO THE HEART OF THE WORLD, LOADED WITH TRUTH, AND UTTERLY TRANSFORMING IN ITS EFFECTS. IT IS A SURE SIGN THAT THERE IS A POWERFUL GOD, THAT HE CAN AND MUST BE APPROACHED THROUGH JESUS CHRIST, AND THAT THERE IS A LIFE BEYOND THE GRAVE WHEN ONE DAY WE SHALL MEET HIM.
> —PETER WALKER[4]

The message of Christ's death and resurrection is a powerful source of hope and new life to millions of people every year. It is easy to miss the evidence of changed lives in a culture where Christians are tempted to complacency and where we are all inundated with bad news at the top of every hour.

FOR FURTHER READING

Etuk, Emma S. *What's So Good about Christianity? Five Amazing Ways the Gospel Has Influenced and Blessed Our Lives.* Washington, D.C. and Uyo, Nigeria: Emida International Publishers, 2000. Nigerian scholar answers the question with passion.

Schmidt, Alvin J. *Under the Influence: How Christianity Transformed Civilization.* Grand Rapids: Zondervan, 2001. The positive impact of Christianity in sexuality, health care, labor, education, science, politics, the abolition of slavery, the arts, and literature.

19

THE EVIDENCE OF THOSE
WHO DIED FOR CHRIST

ONLY CHRIST HAS INSPIRED SO
MANY TO DIE SO NOBLY AS
MARTYRS FOR THEIR FAITH.

The way the followers of Jesus live demonstrates that the life of the

risen Christ is not an abstraction or a mere symbol but a reality. The

same is true for the way Christ's followers die.

According to Jesus himself, His followers would all too often be

hated, mistreated, and even killed as a result—directly or indirectly—of

their stand for Christ. Yet even in this suffering, they would find God's

blessing: "Blessed are you when people insult you and persecute you,

and falsely say all kinds of evil against you because of Me" (Matthew

5:11 NASB). In response, Christ urged His followers to love those who treat them so: "But I say, love your enemies and pray for those who per-secute you" (Matthew 5:44 NASB).

> *Greater love has no one than this, that one lay down his life for his friends. You are My friends if you do what I command you. This I command you, that you love one another. If the world hates you, you know that it has hated Me before it hated you.*
>
> —JESUS (JOHN 15:13-14, 17-18 NASB)

"IF THEY PERSECUTED ME,

THEY WILL ALSO PERSECUTE YOU"

Many religions have inspired people to die—and kill—in battle. Lately, a few cults have inspired their members to commit suicide. Mere zeal is no proof of truth.

Throughout church history, many believers in Jesus Christ have had to choose either to renounce their faith or face suffering and even death. Many believers, like the five missionaries in Ecuador described later in this chapter, have willingly put their lives at risk to take the message of Christ to those who have never heard it. That some people would choose to accept death rather than deny their faith is not by itself strong evidence for the truth of their faith. But the sheer number of believers in Christ who have accepted martyrdom, the long period of time over which Christians have become martyrs, and *the way* they have faced death, all considered together is very impressive evidence. It can only be explained by their unshakable confidence that they, like Jesus, will be raised from the dead.

THE BLOOD OF THE MARTYRS IS SEED.
—Tertullian

The Church has experienced three main periods of intense persecution of its believers. The first period ran from the beginning of the Church's history until the time of Constantine, or roughly the first three centuries. All of the Church's founding apostles except John were martyred. Their willingness to die for their faith is difficult to explain unless they were very sure that Jesus had risen from the dead. As N. T. Wright observes, "If you follow a messiah and he gets killed, you obviously backed the wrong horse."[1] Yet Jesus' disciples continued to "back" Jesus even though He had been publicly executed and even though they were next!

As Christianity became predominantly Gentile in composition, Christians were viewed as superstitious, because of their faith in a crucified God, and disloyal to Rome, because of their refusal to offer sacrifices to Caesar or to acknowledge him as a god. Several emperors sponsored the persecution of Christians. Efforts were made to destroy copies of the Bible. Christians were tortured and killed if they refused to do homage to Caesar. The more Christians were executed, the faster Christianity grew—partly because the believers loved Christ to the point of death and partly, as we pointed out earlier, because they loved each other so much in life.

> ### CHRIST AND CAESAR HAD MET IN THE ARENA, AND CHRIST HAD WON.
> —WILL DURANT[3]

The second period of intense persecution was the late medieval era leading up to the Reformation, when the Inquisition put many Christians to death for expressing their faith in ways that challenged the exclusive authority of the Roman hierarchy. Sadly, when Christian institutions have become powerful, those in charge have often given in to the temptation to abuse that power. The history of such abuses is a sobering reminder that it is useless to put our faith in a religious institution (even a Christian one). Our faith should be in Christ alone.

The third period of intense persecution has been the last century or so, and it continues to this day. Various estimates suggest that some one hundred million Christians were martyred during the twentieth century, mostly in Communist and Islamic nations. Communism is still a serious threat to Christians' physical well-being today in China; on the other hand, the Church in China has thrived under persecution, growing to the tens of millions.

By far the most widespread source of persecution against Christians today is Islam. Hundreds of thousands (at least) of Christians have been killed in the south of Sudan, where government-sponsored terror from the north seeks to impose Islam on the entire nation. Some five hundred churches in Indonesia were destroyed by Muslim extremists in the last decade of the twentieth century. In Pakistan, Islamic blasphemy laws make it illegal to voice criticisms of Islam in the course of evangelism. In many Islamic nations, Christian evangelism is simply illegal, as is the distribution or public possession of Bibles or Christian symbols. In those nations where the Christian population is less than 1 percent, such as in Iran, Saudi Arabia, Afghanistan, Yemen, Turkey, Somalia, and Morocco, the reason invariably is government intimidation.

"You Cannot Do Us Any Real Harm"

Not all persecution of Christians during the past century took place under Communist or Islamic regimes. Christians have suffered for their faith on every continent and in almost every country. What is surprising—and deserves to be viewed as evidence for the reality of Christ—is not merely the number of people who have suffered for Christ but how believers have reacted to that suffering and the life-changing results. Let's consider just one example.

In 1955, five young Christian men and their families went to Ecuador to take the Gospel to an Ecuadorian tribe called the Huaorani (known to outsiders as the Aucas). Jim Elliot was a handsome, strong man who had been a college wrestler; now he went in weakness to show the Huaorani the power of Christ. Ed McCully was his class president and an award-winning orator in college; now he went to speak in halting Huao about Jesus. On January 8, 1956, a group of Huaorani, apparently afraid that these men would attack them as many other white men had, killed Jim, Ed, and three other missionaries. They left behind their wives and nine children, including one not yet born.

The story ran in *Life* and *Time* magazines that year, but the story was far from over. One of the widows, Elisabeth Elliot, stayed in the area and within three years was living with the tribe. The Huaorani allowed Elliot to live with them because they were impressed and confused by the fact that, although the missionaries had brought guns with them, they did not use them to defend themselves in the attack. They learned that the missionaries had come to tell them "about another man, Jesus, who freely allowed His own death to benefit all people." As a result, many Huaorani put their faith in *Wangongi*, the Creator God, who had revealed His love for them in Jesus.[3] As the Huaoroni people came to Christ, their lives changed dramatically for the better. They stopped killing each other. They learned to read and write. Their health improved. Their population, which had dwindled to about two hundred when the missionaries arrived, increased to about a thousand. Had it not been for their new lives in Christ, "the Aucas would have soon followed scores of other Amazonian tribal 'nations' into extinction."[4]

The testimonies of the martyrs (a word that means "witnesses")

bear eloquent witness to the reality of the risen Christ in their lives

(see below).

WORDS OF SOME FAMOUS CHRISTIAN MARTYRS

> EIGHTY AND SIX YEARS HAVE I NOW SERVED CHRIST, AND HE HAS NEVER DONE ME THE LEAST WRONG: HOW THEN CAN I BLASPHEME MY KING AND MY SAVIOR?
>
> —POLYCARP (70-156), BISHOP OF SMYRNA

> YOU CAN KILL US, BUT YOU CANNOT DO US ANY REAL HARM.
>
> —JUSTIN MARTYR (CA. 100-165), CHRISTIAN APOLOGIST

> THAT WHICH I HAVE TAUGHT WITH MY LIPS, I WILL NOW SEAL WITH MY BLOOD.
>
> —JAN HUS (1369-1415), CZECH REFORMER, MARTYRED FOR HIS CRITICISM OF ROMAN CATHOLICISM

> WHEN CHRIST CALLS A MAN, HE BIDS HIM COME AND DIE.
>
> —DIETRICH BONHOEFFER (1906-1945), GERMAN LUTHERAN PASTOR, IMPRISONED AND THEN EXECUTED FOR HIS RESISTANCE TO HITLER[5]

HE IS NO FOOL WHO GIVES WHAT HE CANNOT KEEP TO GAIN WHAT HE CANNOT LOSE.

—JIM ELLIOT (1927-1956), MISSIONARY TO THE HUAORANI IN ECUADOR*

FOR FURTHER READING

Elliot, Elisabeth. *Through Gates of Splendor.* New York: Harper, 1957; rev. ed., Wheaton, Ill.: Tyndale House, 1986. One of the most beloved Christian books of the twentieth century, by the missionary widow who helped lead the violent Huaorani tribe to Christ.

Hefley, James and Marti. *By Their Blood: Christian Martyrs of the 20th Century.* Milford, Mich.: Mott Media, 1979. Massive study arranged by geographical area.

20

THE EVIDENCE OF THE UNIQUENESS OF CHRIST

THE WORLD'S RELIGIONS HAVE NO ONE AND NOTHING TO COMPARE WITH JESUS CHRIST.

All right, you may be thinking, *There is a God. But aren't there many religions that lead to God? Won't any of them do? Why insist on Jesus Christ as the way to know God?*

In this book we have sought to focus on some of the positive evidences for believing that God exists and that He has acted to make His love known to us through His Son, Jesus Christ. Although we have made some references to other religions, our purpose here is not to focus on what is wrong with them but on what is right and true about Christ. Still, to understand the Christian message, it is important to understand what is unique about Christ. We'll try to answer this often contentious question in this concluding chapter.

I am the way, and the truth, and the life;
no one comes to the Father, but by me.
—JESUS (JOHN 14:6)

WHAT'S RIGHT WITH THE WORLD'S RELIGIONS

Christians don't (or at least shouldn't) claim that all of the other religions of the world are wrong in everything they say. Each of the major world religions has true and valuable things to say about the human condition. Much can be learned by studying different religions.

The multiplicity and endurance of religions throughout human history testify to the incorrigibly religious, spiritual nature of human beings. On whatever continent, in whatever century, people recognize their need for God. The persistent universality of the desire to connect with some transcendent reality, some divine power beyond the material, in which life and love and truth and meaning can all be found, is attested in all of the major world religions. Our inner need for God points to God's reality as surely as our need for water would prove that water existed even if we had never seen it, were not sure what it would look like if we ran into it, and could not even agree on what to call it.

Each major religion has a distinctive perspective on life that has some merit to it and is worth considering and exploring.

Hinduism recognizes that the end of our bodily life is not the end of us; it emphasizes that what we do in this life will be carried with us when we die; it acknowledges the transitory character of physical life and affirms that there is something more.

> GIVEN THAT WE HAVE A LIMITED AMOUNT OF TIME
> IN THIS LIFE TO STUDY RELIGIONS,
> WE CAN DISPENSE WITH THOSE THAT OFFER US
> A SECOND CHANCE IN THE AFTERLIFE,
> OR WHICH WILL REINCARNATE US
> IF WE MAKE A MISTAKE IN THIS LIFE,
> OR WHICH PROMISE US THAT ALL WILL BE WELL
> EVENTUALLY NO MATTER HOW WE LIVE NOW.
> PRUDENCE DICTATES THAT WE FIRST OUGHT TO
> CONSIDER THE CLAIMS OF THOSE RELIGIONS WHICH
> SAY THAT EVERYTHING DEPENDS UPON THE
> DECISIONS MADE AND LIVED BY IN THIS LIFE.
> —JOHN A. BLOOM[1]

Buddhism offers a penetrating diagnosis of the human condition: suffering appears to be an incorrigible aspect of human life, and this suffering presupposes our attachment to the belief that we are individuals with needs and wants.

Taoism emphasizes that human beings are not in sync with nature. We don't "go with the flow," so to speak. (The idiom is apropos, since Taoism [pronounced DOW-ism] teaches that there is a force that needs to flow in us as it does in nature. Yes, this does sound a lot like *Star Wars!*) We don't get along with a lot of the animals, we're frustrated by the weather, and we've lost our sense of connection to nature.

Islam has a lot going for it, from a Christian point of view. It recognizes that there is only one God, that He created the world, and that human society is a mess because it isn't based on God's law.

Judaism has even more going for it, according to Christianity. After all, Christians and Jews both regard the Old Testament as Scripture, although Jews don't like that title because they don't accept that there is a New Testament. Evangelical Christianity values Orthodox Judaism for preserving much of the truth of God's revelation in the Old Testament.

So accepting Christ doesn't mean rejecting everything the other religions say. Of course, it does mean taking the position that where those other religions disagree with Christ, they're wrong. More to the point, accepting Christ means recognizing that Christ can do something for you that none of the world's religions or their founders can.

You Can't Get There from Here!

It may seem polite to say that all religions are equally valid, but that won't make it possible to avoid having to choose what to believe and what not to believe. It's true that many religions talk about God and offer paths for reaching God. Still, you can't choose all of them, and it isn't wise to assume that any old (or new) path will do. (To be blunt, some people use the idea of all paths leading to God as an excuse not to take any path at all.)

The problem is that the different religions of the world seem to be talking about different paths that lead to different gods. One religion says that God is the divine force in all of us and points to the path of self-realization. Another religion says that God is a grandfatherly being who just wants us all to be as good as we can. Yet another religion says that there are many gods and that we may pick whatever god we find most helpful. To assert, as many do today, that all of these paths are equally valid is to admit that none of them leads in reality to *God;* rather, they are ways of expressing our religious needs. If we are to make a wise decision, we need to take the truth claims of these different religions seriously and decide which one we really believe.

In a sense, Christianity also is a religion—a human association based on a particular way of dealing with the most fundamental issues of life, death, and meaning. Christianity has doctrines, rituals, and other elements associated with a religion. Yet, paradoxically, Christianity announces that religion is not enough. Religions are human institutions that express fallible human beliefs and values. For that very reason, Christianity points away from religion—even away from itself—to Christ.

What Other Religious Founders Claimed

But what about the other great founders of the world religions? You may be wondering if they made claims about themselves similar to those made by Christ. In fact, all of them insisted that in the end they were not of themselves very important.

The greatest religious figure of the East was a prince of the Shakya clan in India born as Siddhārtha Gautama, sometimes called Shakyamuni (the Shakya sage) but more commonly known as the Buddha (which means the Enlightened One). Our knowledge of his life and teachings is sketchy (there is even debate about the century in which he lived[2]), but it is evident to most historians, and even to most Buddhists, that the religion he started was centered on his teaching and not on him. One of his best known sayings was, "Follow the teaching, not the person"—that is, follow the *dharma*, the truth that he taught about suffering and how to overcome it, rather than trying to follow the person of Gautama the Buddha.[3] As Richard Cohen explains, Buddhists do not even view Gautama as the only buddha; his "nonuniqueness" is crucial to understanding Buddhism.[4] Few historians would disagree with the following assessment of the relation of the Buddha to Buddhism:

One could go so far as to say that as far as the truth of Buddhist teaching is concerned, it does not even matter that much whether the Buddha as a historical personality ever existed, whereas Christianity would lose its meaning without the historical person of Jesus.[5]

Without a doubt the most influential religious leader in world history besides Jesus was Muhammad, the founder of Islam. In the Qur'an, Muhammad confesses, "I am only a mortal, as you are. To me it has been revealed that your God is one God." God tells Muhammad, "Say, 'I am not an innovation among the Messengers, and I know not what shall be done with me or with you. I only follow what is revealed to me; I am only a clear warner.'" Muhammad confesses that he cannot do miracles: "Glory be to my Lord! Am I aught but a mortal, a Messenger?"[6]

Moses, the founder of Judaism, was the ultimate reluctant prophet. The Book of Exodus reports that Moses actually tried to talk the Lord into finding someone else to be His prophet (Exodus 4:10-16)! Moses constantly prefaced his statements to Pharaoh or to the Israelites with the words, "Thus says the LORD." The first time he said these words, Pharaoh responded, "Who is the LORD that I should obey His voice to let Israel go?" (Exodus 5:2 NASB). This captures precisely the spirit of the entire Old Testament, where the main issue is, "Who is the LORD?—whether or not He really is the one true God. The focus of the Old Testament and of Judaism throughout the millennia, is not on the prophets but on God.

JESUS IS THE ANSWER

As we saw in earlier chapters of this book, Jesus Christ was not just one of many pretty-good religious teachers. He was God's only eternal Son, come as a human being to die and rise from the dead. The Buddha, Muhammad, and even Moses are all dead; but Jesus is alive! He offered, not merely a code of ethics or set of religious rituals, but himself as the way for us to be assured of God's mercy.

In this regard Jesus has no competition among the world's religions; He is the only Savior on the market. The Buddha offered himself only as an example of how a human being can rise above suffering through self-enlightenment; even if you think the Buddha was on to something, he cannot help you be reconciled to God. Muhammad claimed only to be the conduit of God's laws by which people ought to order their lives; Islam offers no help to you if you have failed miserably in living up to God's expectations.

By getting to know Christ and believing in Him, we not only know that there is a God, we come to know who He is and to be assured of His eternal love. "God demonstrates His own love toward us, in that while we were still sinners, Christ died for us" (Romans 5:8 NKJV). This is good news you just can't find anywhere else.

FOR FURTHER READING

Lutzer, Erwin W. *Christ Among Other gods: A Defense of Christ in an Age of Tolerance.* Chicago: Moody, 1997. Explains why Jesus Christ is the only Savior.

Zacharias, Ravi. *Jesus among Other Gods: The Absolute Claims of the Christian Message.* Dallas: Word, 2000. Through a series of studies in the Gospel of John, Zacharias shows how Jesus meets human needs like no one else can.

AFTERWORD

In this book we have shared with you what we consider twenty compelling evidences supporting the reasonableness of believing that God exists and that He has made himself known in Jesus Christ. Now that you've heard these evidences, what do you do next? Simply absorbing and even accepting this information is not enough. The existence of God is not an isolated fact to be added to our fund of knowledge trivia, like an answer on *Who Wants to Be a Millionaire?* Now you need to do something with this knowledge. What do you do?

First of all, if you're still uncertain if the God of the Bible exists, you need to work through whatever issues may be sticking points for you. Throughout this book we have offered some suggestions of other books you can read that go into more detail on the various evidences than we can here. You might want to look up one or more of these books if you're having trouble deciding what to think about, say, intelligent design or the resurrection of Jesus. You're also welcome to contact our ministries to seek answers to your questions. At the back of this book you'll find contact information for both of us.

If you're now at the point that you believe in this God, or at least are leaning in that direction, you should start making some concrete, practical response to God. We would encourage you to start talking to God. In religious language this is called "prayer," but many people are skittish about praying because they think they have to speak Elizabethan English or use some formula to get God's attention. Sadly, many people have given up on prayer because they were erroneously taught that prayer is a way of getting God to give you things, and when they tried it they got nothing. Can we be frank with you? We don't believe in God because we get things when we pray. Sometimes God gives us what we ask for; sometimes He doesn't. We pray because we're convinced that God exists and that He wants us to have a relationship with Him. So, our suggestion would be to start talking to God in your own individual, personal way. Tell Him what you believe now; be open about your doubts, questions, or fears. God is real; now is the time to start acting like it!

There are other things you should start doing to cultivate your relationship with God. One of these is to read the Bible, especially the

Gospels, and get to know Christ better. It's also a good idea to get together with others who are also in the process of getting to know God through Jesus Christ; you can help each other. The most obvious place to do that is in a church, but it isn't the only place. Christians can be found meeting together in college dorms, in conference rooms at the office, and at friends' homes for coffee.

Again, we invite you to contact us if we can be of any help as you embark on life's greatest adventure—getting to know God personally through faith in Jesus Christ. As you come to a deep understanding and appreciation for God, your life will change. Who knows—you might be compelling evidence for someone else to believe in God!

ENDNOTES

Foreword

1 Francis Bacon, *Advancement in Learning* (1605), Book 5, Chapter 8.

2 Terry L. Miethe and Gary R. Habermas, *Why Believe? God Exists! Rethinking the Case for God and Christianity* (Joplin, Mo.: College Press, 1993), 9.

Chapter 1

1 C. S. Lewis, "Man or Rabbit?" in *God in the Dock: Essays on Theology and Ethics,* ed. Walter Hooper (Grand Rapids: Eerdmans, 1970), 108-9.

2 Jane Wagner, *The Search for Signs of Intelligent Life in the Universe* (New York: Harper & Row, 1985), 18, quoted in J. Richard Middleton and Brian J. Walsh, *Truth Is Stranger Than It Used to Be: Biblical Faith in a Postmodern Age* (Downers Grove, Ill.: InterVarsity Press, 1985), 29-30.

3 On *Star Trek* as a parable, see Robert M. Bowman Jr., "Strange New Worlds: The Humanist Philosophy of *Star Trek," Christian Research Journal* 14 (fall 1991). On *Star Wars* as a parable, see Bowman, "The Gospel According to Lucas," *Watchman Fellowship's Vantage Point,* fall 1999.

4 The idea of using the Great Pumpkin, Linus's imaginary Halloween hero in the Charles Schultz comic strip *Peanuts,* to illustrate a defective kind of religious faith comes from Christian philosopher Alvin Plantinga's famous essay "Reason and Belief in God" (in *Faith and Rationality: Reason and Belief in God,* ed. Alvin Plantinga and Nicholas Wolterstorff [Notre Dame, Ind.:

University of Notre Dame Press, 1983, 16-93), although we are using the idea in a very different way.

[5] John Warwick Montgomery, *Faith Founded on Fact: Essays in Evidential Apologetics* (Nashville: Thomas Nelson, 1978).

Chapter 2

[1] Thomas S. Kuhn, *The Structure of Scientific Revolutions* (Chicago: University of Chicago Press, 1962, 1970).

[2] Ravi Zacharias, *Jesus Among Other Gods* (Nashville: Word, 2000), 4.

Chapter 3

[1] Carl Sagan, *Cosmos* (New York: Random House, 1980), 4.

[2] Atheists sometimes complain that the word *atheism* means merely the lack of a belief in God, not the belief that no God exists. This isn't correct: the word *atheism*, like the similarly formed words *monotheism, polytheism,* and *pantheism,* refers to a particular view about the world and its relation to the divine, if any. For those stuck on this point, substitute the more cumbersome term *atheistic materialism* wherever we speak of atheism. See further Kenneth D. Boa and Robert M. Bowman Jr., *An Unchanging Faith in a Changing World: Understanding and Responding to Critical Issues That Christians Face Today* (Nashville: Thomas Nelson, 1998), 67-70.

[3] G. K. Chesterton, *Heretics* (New York: John Lane, 1905), 15.

[4] George H. Smith, *Atheism: The Case Against God* (New York: Prometheus Books, 1991), 27.

5 Shirley MacLaine, *Dancing in the Light* (New York: Bantam Books, 1986), 354.

6 Francis J. Beckwith and Stephen E. Parrish, *See the Gods Fall: Four Rivals to Christianity* (Joplin, Mo.: College Press, 1997), 210.

7 William Lane Craig, *Reasonable Faith: Christian Truth and Apologetics* (Wheaton, Ill.: Crossway, 1994), 121.

8 Richard Swinburne, *Existence of God*, rev. ed. (Oxford: Clarendon Press, 1991), 288-289, 291.

Chapter 4

1 Robert Jastrow, *God and the Astronomers* (New York: W. W. Norton, 1978), 46-47, 85-86.

2 Ibid., 27.

3 Hugh Ross, *The Creator and the Cosmos: How the Greatest Scientific Discoveries of the Century Reveal God*, 2d ed. (Colorado Springs: NavPress, 1995), 19.

4 Ibid., 19-29.

5 Stephen W. Hawking, *A Brief History of Time: From the Big Bang to Black Holes*, Introduction by Carl Sagan (New York: Bantam Books, 1988), 174-75.

6 Jastrow, *God and the Astronomers*, 115-16.

Chapter 5

1 *Star Trek III: The Search for Spock*, directed by Leonard Nimoy, produced and written by Harve Bennett (Hollywood: Paramount Pictures, 1984).

[2] Hawking, *Brief History of Time,* 125.

[3] Roger Penrose, *The Emperor's New Mind: Concerning Computers, Minds, and the Laws of Physics,* Foreword by Martin Gardner (New York and Oxford: Oxford University Press, 1989), 339-44.

[4] Hugh Ross, "Design Evidences for Life Support: Probability Estimate for Attaining the Necessary Parameters for a Life Support Planet." Pasadena, Calif.: Reasons to Believe, 2000. Online at www.reasons.org/resources/apologetics/designprobabilityupdate1998.html

[5] Steven Weinberg, *The First Three Minutes* (New York: Basic, 1977), 153.

[6] Peter D. Ward and Donald Brownlee, *Rare Earth: Why Complex Life Is Uncommon in the Universe* (New York: Copernicus—Springer-Verlag, 2000), 37.

[7] Actually, in a lottery no one is guaranteed to win, which is why lottery jackpots are added cumulatively and the game replayed until someone does win.

[8] Stephen W. Hawking, quoted in Fred Hereen, *Show Me God: What the Message from Space Is Telling Us about God;* Wonders That Witness, vol. 1 (Wheeling, Ill.: Searchlight Publications, 1995), 186.

[9] Fred Hoyle, "The Universe: Past and Present Reflections," *Annual Review of Astronomy and Astrophysics 20* (1982) 16.

[10] Charles Townes, *Making Waves* (New York: American Institute of Physics, 1995), cited in Max Jammer, *Einstein and Religion: Physics and Theology* (Princeton: Princeton University Press, 1999), 158.

[11] Paul Davies, *The Cosmic Blueprint: New Discoveries in Nature's Creative Ability to Order the Universe* (New York: Simon and Schuster, 1988), 203.

[12] Ed Harrison, *Masks of the Universe* (New York: Macmillan—Collier Books, 1985), 252.

[13] Richard Morris, *The Fate of the Universe* (New York: Playboy Press, 1982), 154-55, quoted in Hereen, *Show Me God,* 179-80.

[14] Quoted in Sharon Begley, "Science of the Sacred," *Newsweek,* 28 Nov. 1994, 58, as cited in Hereen, *Show Me God,* 184.

[15] Freeman Dyson, *Disturbing the Universe* (New York: Harper & Row, 1979), 250, cited in Hereen, *Show Me God,* 198.

Chapter 6

[1] See Dean L. Overman, *A Case against Accident and Self-Organization* (Lanham, Md.: Rowman & Littlefield, 1997), 31-102; Jonathan Wells, "The Miller-Urey Experiment," Chapter 1 in his *Icons of Evolution: Science or Myth? Why Much of What We Teach about Evolution Is Wrong* (Washington, D.C.: Regnery Publishing, 2000), 9-27, and Wells's extensive endnotes, 263-69.

[2] Ward and Brownlee, *Rare Earth,* 61.

[3] Ibid., xix.

[4] Charles B. Thaxton, Walter L. Bradley, and Roger L. Olsen, *The Mystery of Life's Origin: Reassessing Current Theories* (New York: Philosophical Library, 1984), 66.

[5] On other alternatives to the standard primordial soup theory, see Walter L. Bradley and Charles B. Thaxton, "Information & the Origin of Life," in *The Creation Hypothesis: Scientific Evidence for an Intelligent Creator,* ed. J. P. Moreland (Downers Grove, Ill.: InterVarsity Press, 1994), 173-210 (especially 193-96).

6 Ross, *The Creator and the Cosmos,* 152-53.

7 Quoted in Stephen C. Meyer, "Word Games: DNA, Design, and Intelligence," in *Signs of Intelligence: Understanding Intelligent Design,* ed. William A. Dembski and James M. Kushiner (Grand Rapids: Baker—Brazos Press, 2001), 102.

8 Michael Denton, *Evolution: A Theory in Crisis* (Bethesda, Md.: Adler & Adler, 1986), 235.

9 Ibid., 239.

10 Robert Shapiro, *Origins: A Skeptic's Guide to the Creation of Life on Earth* (New York: Summit Books, 1986), 116.

11 Michael J. Behe, *Darwin's Black Box: The Biochemical Challenge to Evolution* (New York: Free Press, 1996), 172.

12 David Koerner and Simon LeVay, *Here Be Dragons: The Scientific Quest for Extraterrestrial Life* (New York: Oxford University Press, 2000), 241.

13 Hubert Yockey, *Information Theory and Molecular Biology* (New York: Cambridge University Press, 1992), 284. Yockey considers himself an agnostic.

14 Fred Hoyle, *The Intelligent Universe* (London: Michael Joseph, 1983), in Walter L. Bradley and Charles B. Thaxton, "Information and the Origin of Life," in *The Creation Hypothesis,* ed. Moreland, 190-91.

15 Karl Popper, *Unended Quest: An Intellectual Autobiography,* rev. ed. (London: Fontana/Collins, 1976), 168-69, cited in John Ankerberg and John Weldon, in *The Creation Hypothesis,* ed. Moreland, 287.

16 Francis Crick, *Life Itself* (New York: Simon & Schuster, 1981), 88.

Chapter 7

1. William A. Dembski, *Intelligent Design: The Bridge between Science and Theology* (Downers Grove, Ill.: InterVarsity, 1999), 107.

2. Ibid., 106.

3. William A. Dembski, "The Explanatory Filter: A three-part filter for understanding how to separate and identify cause from intelligent design" (Access Research Network, 1998; http://www.arn.org/docs/dembski/wd_explfilter.htm).

4. Stephen C. Meyer, "The Origin of Life and the Death of Materialism," *Intercollegiate Review* 31:2 (April 1, 1996), online, Discovery Institute: Center for the Renewal of Science & Culture (http://www.discovery.org).

5. Dembski develops this filter most fully in his book *The Design Inference: Eliminating Chance through Small Probabilities*, "Cambridge Studies in Probability, Induction, and Decision Theory" (New York: Cambridge University Press, 1998). For shorter introductions, see Dembski, "The Explanatory Filter"; "Signs of Intelligence: A Primer on the Discernment of Intelligent Design," in *Signs of Intelligence*, ed. Dembski and Kushiner, 171-92.

6. This is, of course, a rough estimate that assumes for the sake of simplicity that there may be roughly 20,000 meaningful sentences or phrases that can be formed using twenty letters.

7. The chart here does not come from Dembski, who uses a somewhat different flow chart to convey the same method; see Dembski, "Signs of Intelligence," 182.

8. Michael Behe, "Intelligent Design Theory As a Tool for Analyzing Biochemical Systems," in *Mere Creation: Science, Faith & Intelligent Design*, ed. William A. Dembski (Downers Grove, Ill.: InterVarsity Press, 1998), 178.

9. Ibid.; *Darwin's Black Box: The Biochemical Challenge to Evolution* (New York: The Free Press, 1996), 42; and "A Mousetrap Defended: Reply to Critics" (Access Research Network, 2000), online at http://www.arn.org/docs/behe/mb_mousetrapdefended.htm.

10. Behe, *Darwin's Black Box*, 70-72; "Examples of Irreducible Complexity," Access Research Network Web site, http://www.arn.org/behe/mb_ic.htm.

11. "The Bacterial Flagellum: An Example of Irreducible Complexity," from the Web site of the Faculty/Staff Christian Forum, University of California at Santa Barbara, http://www.id.ucsb.edu/fscf/library/origins/graphics-captions/Flagellum.html.

12. Ibid., 74-97 (quote on p. 97).

13. Ibid., 193.

Chapter 8

1. We discuss the matter from different perspectives in our book *Faith Has Its Reasons: An Integrative Approach to Defending Christianity* (Colorado Springs: NavPress, 2001), 120-23, 140-44, 212-13, 331-34, 348-53, 427-29, 439-43, 528-29. Excellent popular treatments of the question include C. S. Lewis, *The Problem of Pain* (New York: Macmillan, 1943); Norman L. Geisler, *The Roots of Evil* (Grand Rapids: Zondervan, 1978); Peter Kreeft, *Making Sense out of Suffering* (Ann Arbor, Mich.: Servant Books, 1986); William Lane Craig, *No Easy Answers* (Chicago: Moody Press, 1990).

[2] Wendy Northcutt, *The Darwin Awards: Evolution in Action* (New York: Dutton, 2000), 195, 233, 288; see her Web site, http://www.Darwin Awards.com.

[3] Ibid., 2.

[4] Charles Van Doren, *A History of Knowledge: Past, Present, and Future* (New York: Ballantine Books, 1991), 407.

[5] For an interesting Christian perspective on this event, see Robin Jones, *Where Was God at 9:02 A.M.?* (Nashville: Thomas Nelson, 1995).

[6] Russell Yates, as quoted in the *ABC News* report "Yates Gets Life," March 15, 2002, online at http://abcnews.go.com/sections/us/DailyNews/yates-trial020315.html.

[7] The view we are describing here is especially prevalent in Buddhism, though some variation on this approach is common among pantheists.

Chapter 9

[1] Jeffery L. Sheler, *Is the Bible True? How Modern Debates and Discoveries Affirm the Essence of the Scriptures* (San Francisco: Harper; Grand Rapids: Zondervan, 1999), 151.

[2] F. F. Bruce, *The New Testament Documents: Are They Reliable?* 5th rev. ed. (Downers Grove, Ill.: InterVarsity Press, 1960, 1981 printing), 19-20.

[3] Sheler, *Is the Bible True*, 76.

[4] Ian Wilson, *The Bible Is History* (Washington, D.C.: Regnery, 1999), 242.

Chapter 10

[1] Michael D. Lemonick, "Are the Bible's Stories True?" *Time,* Dec. 18, 1995, 69.

[2] "The Admonitions of Ipuwer," Web page of "An Introduction to the History and Culture of Pharaonic Egypt," at http://nefertiti.iwebland.com/texts/ipuwer.htm; see also Francis Hitching, *The Mysterious World: An Atlas of the Unexplained* (New York: Holt, Rinehart and Winston, 1979), 173, for the application of this text to the Exodus.

[3] For an excellent recent discussion of Josephus's references to Jesus, see Robert E. Van Voorst, *Jesus Outside the New Testament: An Introduction to the Ancient Evidence,* "Studying the Historical Jesus" (Grand Rapids: Eerdmans, 2000), 81-104.

[4] On what follows, see Sir William Ramsay, *The Bearing of Recent Discovery on the Trustworthiness of the New Testament* (New York: Hodder and Stroughton, 1915); W. W. Gasque, "The Historical Value of Acts," *Tyndale Bulletin* 40 (1989) 136–57; Gregory A. Boyd, "The Reliability of Acts" (Christus Victor Ministries, 2000), online at http://www.gregboyd.org/gbfront/index.asp?PageID=310.

[5] A. N. Sherwin-White, *Roman Society and Roman Law in the New Testament* (New York: Oxford University Press, 1963), 173.

Chapter 11

[1] For a recent discussion of the interpretation of this passage, see Eugenie Johnston, "The Return of the Jews," in *The Evidence of Prophecy: Fulfilled Prediction as a Testimony to the Truth of Christianity,* ed. Robert C. Newman (Hatfield, Pa.: Interdisciplinary Biblical Research Institute, 1988), 83-97.

[2] Karl Barth, "The Church of Jesus Christ: Sermon on Romans 15:5-13," Bonn, 12 Oct. 1933, *Letter from the Karl Barth Archives* 1 (1998), at http://www.unibas.ch/karlbarth/NewsL98.html. Several versions of this story are told; this one seems to be the most reliable.

[3] Some critics contend that the ruler mentioned in Daniel 9:26 as causing this destruction was Antiochus IV Epiphanes, the Greek king ruling at the time of the Maccabees. However, Antiochus did not destroy the city or the Temple. He did cause considerable damage in storming the city, but far from destroying it, he fortified it as a citadel (1 Macc. 1:31-32). Antiochus also *defiled* the Jewish Temple (he had a pagan sacrifice offered in it), but he did not destroy it.

[4] Except where noted, our quotations from Daniel in the rest of this section are our own literal translations.

[5] Harold W. Hoehner, *Chronological Aspects of the Life of Christ* (Grand Rapids: Zondervan, 1977), 117-18.

[6] Ben Zion Wachholder, "The Calendar of Sabbatical Cycles during the Second Temple and the Early Rabbinic Period," *Hebrew Union College Annual* 44 (1973), 153-96, cited in Robert C. Newman, "The Time of the Messiah," in *The Evidence of Prophecy,* ed. Newman, 117.

[7] Some technical points: (1) There is no year zero between 1 B.C. and A.D. 1. (2) Each cycle starts in the same year that the previous one ended because we are assuming the ancient Hebrew calendar, in which the New Year began sometime in our March or April. (3) A sabbatical cycle that would include the year 445 or 444 B.C. could have started in any year (i.e., any year from 452 to 444) and the 69th cycle would have included the year A.D. 30 or 33 or (in most cases) both. This fact shows that any new discoveries that require revisions to these dates is highly unlikely to affect the outcome.

Chapter 12

[1] Stanley L. Jaki, *Science and Creation* (New York: Academic Press, 1974), 278.

[2] On Copernicus and Galileo, see Boa and Bowman, *Unchanging Faith in a Changing World*, 4-9.

[3] J. H. Tiner, *Johannes Kepler—Giant of Faith and Science* (Milford, Mich.: Mott Media, 1977), quoted in Ann Lamont, "Johannes Kepler (1571-1630)," Creation 15:1 (Dec. 1992-Feb. 1993) 40-43, online at http://www.answersingenesis.org/docs/342.asp.

[4] Thomas Cahill, *The Gifts of the Jews: How a Tribe of Desert Nomads Changed the Way Everyone Thinks and Feels* (New York: Doubleday—Nan A. Talese, 1998), 85.

[5] This is Thomas O. Lambdin's translation, found in James M. Robinson, ed., *The Nag Hammadi Library*, rev. ed. (San Francisco: HarperCollins, 1990), and online at http://www.gnosis.org/naghamm/gthlamb.html. Other translations read basically the same way.

[6] William Foxwell Albright, "Moses in Historical and Theological Perspective," in *Magnalia Dei—The Mighty Acts of God: Essays on the Bible and Archaeology in Memory of G. Ernest Wright*, ed. Frank Moore Cross, Werner E. Lemske, and Patrick D. Miller Jr. (Garden City, N.Y.: Doubleday, 1976), 131.

Chapter 13

[1] Jaraslov Pelikan, *Jesus through the Centuries: His Place in the History of Culture* (New Haven, Conn.: Yale University Press, 1985; reprint, New York: Harper & Row, 1987).

[2] Ibid., 1.

[3] Bruce, *New Testament Documents*, 119.

[4] Philip Schaff, *History of the Christian Church* (Grand Rapids: Eerdmans, 1962 reprint of 1910 ed.), 1:109.

[5] See especially Martin Hengel, *Crucifixion in the Ancient World and the Folly of the Message of the Cross* (Philadelphia: Fortress Press, 1977).

[6] These ten items are all affirmed by historical Jesus scholars of virtually all stripes. See, for example, the lists of core facts about Jesus from E. P. Sanders and N. T. Wright reproduced in Mark Allan Powell, *Jesus as a Figure in History: How Modern Historians View the Man from Galilee* (Louisville, KY: Westminster John Knox Press, 1998), 117, 153, which agree on all ten of these facts (#2 is implicit in both lists). We are not aware of any historical Jesus scholars who dispute any of these ten facts.

[7] Tom Wright, The Original Jesus: *The Life and Vision of a Revolutionary* (Grand Rapids: Eerdmans, 1996), 84-85.

[8] For what follows, see Boa and Bowman, *Unchanging Faith in a Changing World*, 281-83.

Chapter 14

[1] Philip Yancey, *The Jesus I Never Knew* (Grand Rapids: Zondervan, 1995), 14-15.

[2] George Carey, *God Incarnate: Meeting the Contemporary Challenges to a Classic Christian Doctrine* (Downers Grove, Ill.: InterVarsity Press, 1978), 11.

[3] C. S. Lewis, *Mere Christianity* (New York: Macmillan, 1952; reprint, San Francisco: Harper, 2001), 56; cf. "What Are We to Make of Jesus Christ?" in *God in the Dock,* (Grand Rapids, MI: Wm B. Eerdmans Publishing, 1983), 156-160.

[4] C. S. Lewis, *Miracles: A Preliminary Study* (New York: Macmillan, 1947), 113.

[5] Peter Kreeft and Ronald K. Tacelli, *Handbook of Christian Apologetics: Hundreds of Answers to Crucial Questions* (Downers Grove, Ill.: InterVarsity, 1994), 169.

[6] The chart is taken from Boa and Bowman, *Faith Has Its Reasons,* 127. See also Kreeft and Tacelli, *Handbook of Christian Apologetics,* 165, 171. Kreeft and Tacelli use the terms *Lord, liar, lunatic, guru,* and *myth* to designate the five alternatives.

Chapter 15

[1] John Dominic Crossan, *Who Killed Jesus? Exposing the Roots of Anti-Semitism in the Gospel Story of the Death of Jesus* (San Francisco: Harper, 1995), 5.

[2] For an excellent analysis of these extrabiblical sources for the life and death of Jesus, see F. F. Bruce, *Jesus and Christian Origins outside the New Testament* (Grand Rapids: Eerdmans, 1974).

[3] Hengel, *Crucifixion* (see chap. 13, n. 5).

[4] Some Muslims cite the so-called Gospel of Barnabas as documentary evidence for the view that Judas was crucified in Jesus' place. However, this apocryphal gospel dates from medieval times and has no historical credibility. See Norman L. Geisler, *Baker Encyclopedia of Christian Apologetics,* Baker Reference Library (Grand Rapids: Baker, 1999), 67-69.

5   Hugh Schonfield, *The Passover Plot: A New Interpretation of the Life and Death of Jesus* (New York: Bantam, 1965). Schonfield's book was later made into a feature film of the same title (1975); the role of Jesus was played by Zalman King, who went on to become one of the most successful producers of soft pornography!

6   Michael Baigent, Henry Lincoln, and Richard Leigh, *Holy Blood, Holy Grail* (New York: Dell, 1983).

7   Barbara Thiering, *Jesus the Man* (New York: Doubleday, 1975); see N. T. Wright's discussion in his book *Who Was Jesus?* (Grand Rapids: Eerdmans, 1992), 19-36 (especially 32-34).

8   David Strauss, *A New Life of Jesus* (Eng. trans., 1879), quoted in Ian Wilson, *Jesus: The Evidence: The Latest Research and Discoveries* (San Francisco: Harper San Francisco, 1996), 151.

Chapter 16

1   Gerd Lüdemann, *The Resurrection: History, Experience, Theology,* trans. John Bowden (Minneapolis: Fortress, 1994), 37-44.

2   John Dominic Crossan, *The Historical Jesus: The Life of a Mediterranean Jewish Peasant* (San Francisco: HarperSanFrancisco, 1991), 392-93.

3   John Dominic Crossan, *Jesus: A Revolutionary Biography* (San Francisco: HarperSanFrancisco, 1994), 158.

4   The issue of the relationships among the Gospels of Matthew, Mark, and Luke (called the Synoptic Gospels) continues to be debated. The overwhelming majority view among New Testament scholars is that Mark was written first and that Matthew and Luke drew their material partly from

Mark and partly from an unknown source (either a well-defined oral tradi-
tion or a written document), which has been dubbed "Q." On this compli-
cated question, see especially Robert H. Stein, *Studying the Synoptic Gospels:
Origin and Interpretation,* 2d ed. (Grand Rapids: Baker, 2001); David Alan
Black and David Beck, eds., *Rethinking the Synoptic Problem* (Grand Rapids:
Baker, 2001).

5 This is so, regardless of whether or not one thinks John was *familiar* with the
Synoptics.

6 Pheme Perkins, *Resurrection: New Testament Witness and Contemporary
Reflection* (Garden City, N.Y.: Doubleday, 1984), 94.

7 Craig has discussed this matter in several writings; see especially William
Lane Craig, *Assessing the New Testament Evidence for the Historicity of the
Resurrection of Jesus,* Studies in the Bible and Early Christianity, Vol. 16
(Lewiston, N.Y.: Edwin Mellen Press, 1989), 207-222.

8 Pinchas Lapide, *The Resurrection of Jesus: A Jewish Perspective* (London: SPCK,
1984), 95.

Chapter 17

1 One of the best studies on this matter is John Wenham, *Easter Enigma: Do the
Resurrection Accounts Contradict One Another?* 2d ed. (Grand Rapids: Baker,
1993).

2 Ian Wilson, *Jesus: The Evidence,* 147.

3 All quotations in the table are from the NASB.

4 Reginald H. Fuller, *The Foundations of New Testament Christology* (New York:
Scribners, 1965), 142.

⁵ Michael Grant, *Jesus: An Historian's Review of the Gospels* (New York: Charles Scribner's Sons, 1977), 176.

⁶ E. P. Sanders, *The Historical Figure of Jesus* (London: Penguin Press, 1993), 280.

⁷ On this important point of agreement, see Craig, *Assessing the New Testament Evidence*, 230-47.

⁸ John does not state explicitly that Jesus actually ate the fish. However, he says that Jesus invited the disciples to join Him at His charcoal fire, where He already had fish and bread waiting, and says that Jesus spoke to Peter "when they had finished breakfast" (John 21:9, 15 NASB). In context this seems to mean that Jesus ate breakfast with Peter and the other disciples present.

⁹ On this point, see Robert M. Bowman Jr., *Jehovah's Witnesses,* Zondervan Guide to Cults and Religious Movements (Grand Rapids: Baker, 1995), 42-43.

¹⁰ See especially Murray J. Harris, *From Grave to Glory: Resurrection in the New Testament: Including a Response to Norman L. Geisler* (Grand Rapids: Zondervan—Academie, 1990), 31-79.

¹¹ N. T. Wright, in *The Meaning of Jesus: Two Visions,* by N. T. Wright and Marcus Borg (London: SPCK, 1999), 124.

Chapter 18

¹ Rodney Stark, *The Rise of Christianity* (New York: Harper, 1996).

² See Jimmy Williams, "The Social and Historical Impact of Christianity" (Richardson, Tex.: Probe Ministries, 2000), at http://www.probe.org/docs/soc-impact.html.

³ Rochunga Pudaite, *The Greatest Book Ever Written* (Hannibal, Mo.: Hannibal Books, 1989), 1-10.

⁴ Peter Walker, *The Weekend That Changed the World: The Mystery of Jerusalem's Empty Tomb* (Louisville, Ky.: Westminster John Knox Press, 2000), 193.

Chapter 19

¹ Wright, *The Original Jesus*, 70.

² Will Durant, *The Story of Civilization* (1944), 3:652.

³ Steve Saint, "A Cloud of Witnesses," in *Martyrs: Contemporary Writers on Modern Lives of Faith*, ed. Susan Bergman (San Francisco: HarperSanFrancisco, 1996), 142-54; see also Elisabeth Elliot, *The Savage, My Kinsman* (New York: Harper & Row, 1961).

⁴ Pudaite, *Greatest Book Ever Written*, 101.

⁵ Dietrich Bonhoeffer, *The Cost of Discipleship* (New York: Macmillan, 1961), 99.

⁶ As quoted in Elisabeth Elliot, *Through Gates of Splendor* (New York: Harper, 1957), 172.

Chapter 20

¹ John A. Bloom, "Truth Via Prophecy," in *Evidence for Faith: Deciding the God Question*, ed. John Warwick Montgomery; Cornell Symposium on Evidential Apologetics, 1986 (Dallas: Probe Books, 1991; distributed by Word Publishing), 175.

[2] Sri Lankan sources date Gautama's life to ca. 566-486 B.C., while Indian and Chinese sources indicate that he lived ca. 488-368 B.C.

[3] Quoted in Hans Küng, "The Historical Buddha: His Teaching as a Way to Redemption: 2. A Christian Response," in *Christianity and the World Religions: Paths of Dialogue with Islam, Hinduism, and Buddhism*, by Hans Küng, with Josef van Ess, Heinrich von Stietencrom, and Heinz Bechert (Garden City, N.Y.: Doubleday, 1986), 314.

[4] Richard S. Cohen, "Shakyamuni: Buddhism's Founder in Ten Acts," in *The Rivers of Paradise: Moses, Buddha, Confucius, Jesus, and Muhammad as Religious Founders*, ed. David Noel Freedman and Michael J. McClymond (Grand Rapids: Eerdmans, 2001), 133.

[5] Heinz Bechert, "The Historical Buddha: His Teaching As a Way to Redemption: 1. Buddhist Perspectives," in *Christianity and the World Religions*, by Küng, et. al., 294.

[6] Sura 41:6; 46:9; 17:93; quoted in Josef van Ess, "Muhammad and the Qur'an: Prophecy and Revelation: 1. Islamic Perspectives," in *Christianity and the World Religions*, by Küng, et. al., 13.

Afterword

[1] C. S. Lewis, "Is Theology Poetry?" in *The Weight of Glory*, rev. and expanded ed. (New York: Macmillan, 1980), 92.

About the Authors

Kenneth D. Boa is the president of Reflections Ministries, an organization that seeks to provide safe places for people to consider the claims of Christ and to help them mature and bear fruit in their relationship with Him:

Reflections Ministries
One Piedmont Center, Suite #130
Atlanta, Georgia 30305
http://www.reflectionsministries.org

Robert M. Bowman Jr., is the president of Apologetics.com, which focuses on providing people with reasons for faith in Christ and answers to questions about the truth of Scripture:

Apologetics.com, Inc.
P.O. Box 60511
Pasadena, California 91116
http://www.apologetics.com

Additional copies of this book and other
titles from RiverOak Publishing
are available from your local bookstore.

If you have enjoyed this book,
or if it has impacted your life,
we would like to hear from you.

Please contact us at:

RiverOak Publishing
Department E
P.O. Box 55388
Tulsa, Oklahoma 74155

Visit our website at:
www.riveroakpublishing.com